Paul Kennedy is an ABC television presenter with twenty-five years' journalistic experience. He is the author of four previous books, including *Hell on the Way to Heaven* (co-authored with Chrissie Foster), which helped Australian survivors of child sex abuse achieve the nation's largest Royal Commission. Paul is also a successful football coach on the Mornington Peninsula. He lives in Seaford, Victoria, with his wife and three sons.

funkytown
PAUL KENNEDY

Affirm press

First published by Affirm Press in 2021
28 Thistlethwaite Street, South Melbourne,
Boonwurrung Country, VIC 3205
affirmpress.com.au
10 9 8 7 6 5 4 3 2 1

Every effort has been made to trace copyright holders and to obtain their
permission for the use of copyright material. The publisher apologises for
any errors or omissions and would be grateful if notified of any corrections
that should be incorporated in the final printed edition or future editions and
reprints of this book.

Title: Funkytown / Paul Kennedy, author
ISBN: 9781922419828 (paperback)

 A catalogue record for this
book is available from the
National Library of Australia

Cover design by Luke Causby, Blue Cork
Cover photograph by AAP Image/Ben Macmahon
Typeset in Granjon 12/17.5 pt by J&M Typesetting
Proudly printed in Australia by Griffin Press

For Joan and Mick, who gave us everything. And for my wife Kim, with love and thanks.

Some names in this book have been changed to protect the privacy of old friends and acquaintances.

Contents

PART ONE   **1**

1   Drinking the Rain   3

2   Outside The Grand   15

3   Under the Pergola   25

4   Mrs Mac   33

5   The Shrink   41

6   Thinking About Drinking   45

7   Racing Quadzilla   49

8   The Pier   59

9   Moving Shadow   61

10   'Give it Your Best'   69

11   The First Game   75

12   Mum in Black and White   89

13   Making a Buck   97

14   Dick Togs   103

15   Sam and Me   107

16   The Club   115

17   Dad's Footsteps   125

18   Getting Away with it   127

19   Clueless   131

20   Jobless   133

21   Owl Calls   135

22   The Cut   139

23   Sweet Spots   147

24   The Killer Returns   151

PART TWO   **155**

25   Night Rider   157

26   The Call   161

27   A Saint   165

28   Another Chance   173

29   Bad Feeling   183

30   A Different Story   187

31   Curfew   191

32   Captain Seahorse   193

33   Speaking Out   199

34   Boys Fought   203

35   A Poke in the Eye   213

36   Who's Got the Petrol?   217

37   Natalie   221

38   Whitey's Tears   225

39   Taxi to Nowhere   229

40   At Last   237

41   Almost Spiritual   239

42   Milestone   243

43   The Big Stage   245

44   Lessons Learnt   255

45   Soundtrack of My Youth   259

46   Mucking Up   263

47   Any Questions?   269

48   Unwanted   273

49   Apologies   277

50   Nothing to Lose   281

51   Fond Farewells   287

52   Where Does the Water Go?   291

53   Laughing Gear   297

Epilogue   301

Acknowledgements   307

'All of childhood's unanswered questions must finally be
passed back to the town and answered there.'
Maya Angelou, *I Know Why the Caged Bird Sings*, 1969

'Don't mess with the bull, young man,
you'll get the horns.'
Mr Vernon, *The Breakfast Club*, 1985

part one

1

Drinking the Rain

Backyard birdcalls and a streak of summer sun crept into my room to wake me, making me squint. It was January 1993. The first day of my final year of school. I was seventeen. I kicked off my sweat-damp sheet with a sigh, rolled off my single bed onto the carpet, and started doing push-ups. In my cheap elastic jocks, elbows tucked, eyes up, arse down, counting.

More than anything, I wanted to play football under lights at the Melbourne Cricket Ground. Push-ups were going to help me get there. Often, I pictured myself running, bouncing, twisting one way then another, a record crowd standing to applaud my courage and skill. Every night I fell asleep in that room I had the same visions, only they were in silent slow-motion. This was my last chance to turn ambition into reality. Most recruits got drafted into the Australian Football League when they were seventeen. This was my big year, and I knew it. What I didn't know was just how momentous it would be.

We lived in Seaford, two train stops from Frankston. There were plenty of nicknames for Frankston. Franger. Frangalas (after a 1980s footballer). I'm sure there were others, but my favourite was the one my little sister Kate used: Funkytown. She always said it with a cheeky smile. The city was more than forty kilometres away. Not that we cared. In Funkytown, we had it all: a Myer, two surf shops, a double-storey Macca's, and a popcorn cinema with a magical domed ceiling that changed colour every few seconds. The ever-expanding shopping district had an American-style mall – a singular high-rise building so ugly it was quaint – a Brashs music store, a Pancake Parlour, a rotating dance floor nightclub, and an annual foreshore circus with caged African lions. Above it all was the lookout at Oliver's Hill, where you could linger on the expanse of Port Phillip, a majestic bay with as many moods and secrets as an ocean.

At fifty push-ups I stopped, turned onto my back and did crunches till my stomach burned with pain. With arms and legs stretched out, I let my pulse return to normal. Then I went to the mirror on my wall and admired my torso. A plaster cast covered my left hand like an oversized glove. My skin was itching under it, but I knew the bone was healing because the aching had stopped. I didn't want to think about how I'd broken my hand. I just wanted it fixed. Another week or so and I'd be able to cut the bloody cast off.

I checked in the mirror for pimples on my chin. My skin was hardening from fortnightly shaving, but I still got the odd whitehead. If one appeared, I squeezed it hard to send a message to others. I ran my fingers through my wiry hair, which I'd started to grow long. Until this year I'd only ever had a short back and sides, trimmed straight as a ruler across my forehead, like a Lego man. Mum used to cut our hair. She learnt how to do it from a *Women's Weekly* article. The four of us Kennedy kids weren't prima donnas: we didn't request anything fancy, although after seeing *Top Gun* in

1986 I begged for a Maverick hairdo. Mum rolled her eyes and cut off my fringe altogether. My older sister, Jo, said it made me look simple and nothing whatsoever like Tom Cruise. I wore a hat and a frown for a month.

'You'd better hurry up,' Mum called to me from the kitchen. 'Don't wanna be late first day back.'

She was wrapping a sandwich when I came out of my room. She wore a green shirt, gold earrings, and a necklace so long she looped it twice around.

'You look nice,' I told her.

'Thanks love.' She kissed me on the cheek. 'I gotta go to work. Love you.'

She strode down the hall and I heard the front door bang shut behind her.

I made myself breakfast: seven Vita Brits and milk. We only ever had skinny milk in our house. I drank it like water, often straight from the carton when no one was watching.

The house was unusually tranquil and spacious. I'd been noticing things like this recently. My family home was changing. It used to be busy and full. Now, it was as if it didn't belong to me as much as it used to, or I had started to outgrow it. In my diary I called it a growing restlessness. I also suspected I was becoming nostalgic.

For five months I'd been filling pages of a school notebook with my thoughts. The entries had begun when a girl from school dumped me. Louise King. This led me to writing about other things – prospects beyond high school, short stories and movie quotes. I wrote slowly to make it last, hovering my pen over the page at the beginning of new sentences and paragraphs, crossing out some words to replace them with something more specific and honest. I wrote about my feelings. It felt like a cure for some undiagnosed ailment.

I stuffed my schoolbooks into my backpack and rode my bike to my best friend's house. I could get there in two minutes if I fanged it. Adam Ray lived on the corner of East and Downs Roads, one of the main intersections in our estate. I bunny-hopped up the gutter, squeezed my brakes and jumped off, flinging my bike on his lawn. The handlebars jackknifed against the frame and the back wheel kept spinning. Luke, the Ray family dog, was watching me through the loungeroom window.

'Sorry, I'm late,' I said, bounding through the door.

'Sure you are.' There was no need to shake hands in reunion. We'd spent most of the six-week summer holidays together.

The two of us had been mates since kindergarten, back in the days when he used to make faces and chew warts off his knees. He was a good-looking kid with blue eyes, freckles and wavy red hair – a real-life Ginger Meggs. He used to get teased for his hair colour. 'Carrot top' was just one of the names he copped, and hated. 'Carrot tops are green, so there,' he used to tell his tormentors in primary school. These days, he didn't get sledged much at all. He had a quick temper and a decent right cross if needed. He also had his father's natural barrel chest and strong arms. Which is not to say he was a brawler. He'd tell a joke rather than raise a fist. He was thoughtful, too. When I broke my collarbone playing junior footy he came around to my house with a Polly Waffle. He'd only eaten half of it by the time he arrived.

'Righto,' Adam said, filling his bag with textbooks. 'Let's get this over and done with.'

He wasn't a keen student. He was a good athlete but didn't live for sport like I did. Adam wanted to be a rock star. He was always singing some new pop song he'd heard on Casey Kasem's *American Top 40 Countdown* on Sunday nights. Adam liked finding out about new bands. Once, he got all giddy about an English group called Bros, and its song 'When Will I Be Famous?' I reckoned he thought the lyrics were written for him.

Adam's singing ambition was no pie in the sky – he had a beautiful voice. Out and about on our various adventures, he would strike up a tune while I did my best to sing back-up. Show me the old Melways street directory and I can trace for you our drunken songlines up this street, down that one, looking for the next party. We were on Map 99 – a sapling housing estate built on an ancient swamp, home to young families and dwindling numbers of frogs.

We had moved here from the country town of Puckapunyal when I was two, in 1977. Dad had quit the army, and the government was offering cheap land under a veterans' resettlement scheme. My parents got a $25,000 loan on a special interest rate. Ours was one of the first houses in the street – Emanuel Drive. Mum took a lot of photos while the house was going up in the otherwise empty expanse. I'm in a few of the shots, standing beside a stack of bricks, dressed in red tartan pants, the weight of my enormous head almost tipping me over. I've been big-headed since day one; young mothers apparently commented on it in the Seymour Hospital ward: 'Look at the size of that one's head. I'm glad he's not mine.'

Adam and I took off, riding in the middle of the road, no hands, cruising. School was about five kilometres away. We rode our treadlies everywhere in those days, in all weather. I especially loved riding through thunderstorms. I used to tilt my head back, stick out my tongue and drink the rain.

'What'd you get up to last night?' I asked Adam as we pedalled.

'Went round to Emma's house,' he said. He and Emma had been going out for a few weeks. She was one of the most popular girls at school. Smart, funny, friendly. Long, blonde curls.

'How long d'ya reckon you'll go out with her?'

'I dunno, why?' he said. 'Don't you like her?'

'Yeah, I do. She's nice.' I was jealous of them. 'Just wouldn't want a girlfriend if I was you. Better off hangin' out with the boys.'

Adam smiled. 'Don't worry, mate. There's someone out there for you too.'

Unlike me, Adam had always found it easy to talk to girls. I was hopeless. In Grade 4, we both had a crush on a girl called Amanda. I tried to impress her by wearing my best BMX T-shirt and Sprintz sneakers, and by doing flips off five-metre parallel bars. Adam had a better plan: he just talked to her, made her laugh. They started going out. I pretended I didn't care.

At Friday night Blue Light Discos, run by the local police, Adam was our John Travolta. We were twelve on our first time. I wore a T-shirt tucked into my rolled-up acid wash jeans, with white cricket shoes. My palms were slippery with sweat. There was a rumour a girl called Kara had agreed to kiss me. She hadn't yet arrived. Adam and I were on the dance floor. He was gyrating. I was swaying, trying to find the beat. There were songs by Starship and The Bangles. In my pre-kiss panic, I worried: 'What if my breath stinks?'

Adam, walking like an Egyptian, agreed I might have a problem. 'But there's nothin' you can do about it now.'

'I could wash me mouth out with soap in the dunnies.'

He grinned. 'Bloody oath,' he said. 'I'll help ya.'

He followed me into the toilets, shaking his head as I lathered up my gums. The kiss never happened – maybe Kara was tipped off. 'You're a dickhead,' Adam kept saying. 'I thought you were joking.' Sometimes it felt good to be a dickhead, even if you were spitting up soap for days afterwards.

To get to school we rode slowly over the graffitied freeway overpass. On the other side, we took the swamp track through the older part of Seaford. The swamp was a heritage-listed wetland that ran along the coast behind a dozen streets of houses. We'd learnt a bit about it in history classes. For thousands of years this was the hunting grounds of the Kulin nation's Boon Wurrung people. The Indigenous name for the area was Carrum-Carrum. In the late 19th century, Europeans built a river nearby. They drained most of the land and subdivided it, preserving only a section of natural habitat: Seaford Swamp. I'd heard adults call it an environmental treasure, a home to rare migratory birds from Asia and beyond. But I wasn't impressed. The place smelled like duck shit and mud. My youthful eyes weren't trained to see its rich colours and soft reflections. I just knew it bred armies of mozzies after big rains, and that some kids reckoned flashers liked hiding out in the tall reeds.

Adam and I had travelled along that swamp track hundreds, maybe thousands, of times, lost in conversations about nothing in particular. Like old men, we talked about friends, family, the weather, or news of the day, especially if it related to our neighbourhood.

About this time there was a crime story on television that had mentioned Seaford. We always got excited when our otherwise anonymous suburb got talked about on TV. But this one took some of the shine off our corner of utopia. Channel Nine reported that someone had broken into a woman's home, not far from our estate, and slaughtered three cats. They had written death threats on the walls in blood. The police talked about the disturbing way in which the animals had been cut up, with their intestines spread over the floor. The cat killer decorated one of the corpses with the picture of a naked woman. The woman whose pets were butchered wasn't there when it happened. Anxious about an earlier prank telephone call, she'd gone with her boyfriend on his pizza delivery run, taking her baby with her. Adam and I wondered if she'd stayed home that night whether she would have been murdered. Adam pointed out that the crime scene was only a few hundred metres from his work. He was a cashier at the popular service station Food Plus.

We rolled up to school after the first bell. Predictably, we weren't the only ones running late. A crowd of students behind a wire fence was looking at the charred remains of the science wing, across the road from the teachers' car park. A month earlier, someone had torched ten computer rooms.

'Fuckin' hell,' one of the kids said.

We had read about it on the front page of the *Herald Sun*: 'School Blaze Agony'. A photo showed our two cleaners, Kim and Dennis, standing next to the crime scene.

'Wonder who did it,' someone said.

'Bet it's someone who goes here.'

I was sure the cops would pinch someone for it. But I never heard anything else about the investigation. We'd get used to the smell of ashes – and make do without computers for a while.

'Hey, you!' I turned to see who was shouting. There was a uniformed policeman across the road, pointing at me. 'Come 'ere.'

I did as instructed.

'Where's ya helmet?' the cop said.

'Shit.' I patted my bare head. I wasn't wearing one.

Adam tapped his skid lid and laughed. 'See ya later, mate,' he said, riding for the bike shed.

My helmet, one of those bulbous yellow Stackhats, was stashed in a cupboard at home. I'd stopped wearing it because it made me look like a dork. I figured it was my head, my risk.

'Got any identification?' the cop said.

'Don't think so.'

'What about a concession card?' He was young and surprisingly affable. If it wasn't for his uniform, I might've liked him.

'Left it at home,' I said.

I was wary of cops.

Two years earlier I'd been caught up in a wrongful arrest. I was walking to the bus stop when a patrol car skidded beside me; two officers sprung out and bent me over their bonnet. It was in the middle of winter and I had the flu, so I was wearing a heavy coat, scarf, beanie and gloves. This apparently made me look like a burglar they'd been chasing around the neighbourhood.

'You've been seen jumpin' fuckin' fences,' one of them said, pushing his entire weight onto my back.

'Nah, ya got the wrong guy.' My hands were pinned. A bolt of pain shot through my shoulders and neck. 'I live round the corner.' They took me home and soon realised their mistake. I said they owed me an apology, but they refused, even after Mum made an official complaint at Frankston police station.

'Never be afraid to speak up against things like that,' Mum told me. I'd never seen her so angry. Injustice made her furious. 'Even the police need to be held accountable for their actions sometimes.'

I got over it – it was no Rodney King moment – but I guess it left a chip on my shoulder.

'We're gunna give you a fine for not wearing a helmet,' the friendly cop was saying. 'If you can't prove who you say you are, I'm gunna have to go and see your principal so he can tell me your name and address.'

'Wait,' I said. 'What about my school diary? That has my name in it. Will that do?'

'That's fine.'

I dug around in my bag for the small green book. The cop started making small talk.

'What year are you in?'

'Twelve.'

'What are ya hoping to do after high school?'

'Lawyer,' I said. 'Reckon I'd be a good barrister. That's if I don't play footy for Collingwood.'

The cop smirked.

'Here it is,' I said.

I showed him my diary. I'd written a fake name and address on the cover. I'd anticipated a moment like this. It might also be handy if I got caught without a ticket on public transport.

The cop read my name: 'William Wyatt.'

'Most people call me Billy,' I said.

'You should start wearing a helmet, Billy. Fifteen bucks is fifteen bucks. Sign here.'

I scribbled a signature. He handed me the fine, keeping a copy for himself. We said our goodbyes.

I was sweating from the humid summer air when I arrived at my classroom for first period. Ten minutes later, it was more of a cold sweat. The public announcement system crackled: 'Paul Kennedy, come to the office, please. Paul Kennedy to the office right away.' I glanced at the fine. I'd signed my real name. 'Shit.' Other students saw my reaction and laughed.

The cop was waiting for me in the principal's office.

'Good try,' he said, handing me another fine with my real name and address. 'Who's Billy Wyatt?'

The principal and a senior teacher stood silently, glaring at me.

'It's a character from one of my favourite movies,' I said. 'You seen *Stealing Home*? It's got Jodie Foster in it.'

'No,' he said. 'I'll look out for the video. Good luck with your studies. Might see you in court one day.'

2

Outside The Grand

The false name I gave the cop wasn't my only lie. When he'd asked about my plaster cast, I'd told him I'd busted my hand in a skateboarding accident. The truth was uglier than that. It was wrapped up in another lie; a lie to myself. While I was dreaming of becoming a football star this year, I was also on my way to becoming an under-age booze hound.

With the help of a fake ID, I was becoming a regular at The Grand Hotel in Frankston. I'd been slipping into this new world for months. It felt daunting and brazen. There were beautiful women everywhere. The throbbing music shifted the crowd this way and that. People were shouting and laughing, almost howling. When I first started going, I stuck close to my brother Steve and his mates, who seemed popular, confident and strong. I was a wide-eyed witness to the way they played pool and threw their empties against the concrete floor; the way they leaned in close to chat up girls, while eye-balling any potential rivals. I wanted to be one of the boys. Seeing me with a beer in the corner, Steve's friends would pat me on the head and tell me I was 'the man', as if I was being anointed, or at least included.

I wound up wearing the plaster cast after another big night

at The Grand with my brother Steve and his mates. It was late on a Saturday, just before Christmas. The pub's security guard had finished hosing down the front steps and locking the doors. There were about two dozen of us milling on the footpath. All the women had gone home.

I'd often got stranded on the street after hours like this, with Steve, his friends and all the other stragglers. It was well known to locals that cabbies stayed away from Frankston's four-pub intersection at this hour. Too much could go wrong. The small fares weren't worth the threat of violence, verbal abuse and vomit.

On this night, every other business on the highway was shut except for Uncle Vic's, the fish and chip shop next to The Grand. Uncle Vic, who worked in the shop with his bull-chested nephews, was famous for giving free dim sims to anyone who reached over the bain-marie and slapped him a spirited high five.

Inevitably, an argument broke out on the footpath, not far from where Steve and I were standing.

'Here we go,' Steve said. 'Bit of action.'

Two young men were closing in on each other, trading insults.

'Fuck you,' said the shorter one.

'Nah, fuck you,' said the other.

'Why don't ya 'ave a go?'

'You 'ava a go, cunt.'

Not quite a debate; more like two dogs barking at each other. I didn't hear the substance of their dispute. I assumed any grievance began inside the hotel earlier. In these street fights, the combatants usually knew each other. The pub crowd was tribal; most boys becoming men were attached to local footy clubs. You became known as a Seaford boy, a Pines boy (Frankston North), a Karingal boy (Frankston East), a Langwarrin boy (a little further east) or a Mt Eliza boy (Frankston South). There were other subtleties, but the point was that local clans fought other local clans. Conflict came from bruised egos or threatened status.

The shorter man happened to be a friend of Steve's. His nickname was Slugger, which wasn't ironic, rather it was an evolution of a previous name: Plugger, after his footballing hero Tony Lockett. Some nicknames had long histories I didn't always understand.

My brother edged as close as he dared, eager to see what would happen next. I followed. Slugger threatened to put the other guy 'to sleep'; he was drunk and fearless and over-confident. The stand-off didn't seem too menacing. I thought it might end in some harmless grappling. But my thinking changed when eight or nine strangers walked around the corner to join the ranks of interested onlookers. The newcomers were in their early twenties; they seemed alert, eager.

I knew only one reason why interlopers came to Frankston at this hour. They wanted to see blood spilled.

I nudged Steve. 'These blokes are gunna jump in,' I said. My brother agreed but seemed unalarmed.

The strangers were whispering to each other. I moved to the front steps of the hotel to get a better view of the crowd. My mouth was dry and I started chewing hard on my fingernails. Slugger and the other guy had stopped shouting at each other. They were glancing the way of the new arrivals. A strange silence fell over the scene. I could hear the seagulls squawking in the trees along the median strip. I saw their white feathers under the streetlights; they were irritating me. It was as if someone had pulled the pin on a grenade, and we were waiting for the explosion.

I'd thought this night might come, my first all-in. In the picture of bravado I'd framed for myself, I was decisive and powerful. All I knew about street-fighting was what I'd seen on action movies with Sly and Arnie and Chuck and Bruce. When the time came for my first go at it, I fantasised about being as tough as those guys. Of course, my Hollywood heroes taught me nothing of violence in the real world. That had mostly come through football. When I was eleven, I lined up an opposition player just to see what it would feel like. We slammed into each other, collapsing in a heap on the grass. The other boy was hurt; I heard all the air leave his body at once. I was also winded but recovered quicker. Dad commented after the game that it looked like one of those hits that made your back teeth rattle.

'I remember that feeling,' he said, recalling his days playing rugby league in Sydney. 'Did it hurt?'

'Yeah,' I said. 'But I'm okay.'

He beamed with pride. Dad was a gentleman, but he couldn't betray his admiration for pain tolerance. I resolved to always be a player praised by my father for his physical courage. I sought out collisions as a way of proving myself. If I got hurt, so be it. I told myself that wilful aggression was in my nature; it came with competitiveness. By the time I was fifteen, rough play often sparked on-field scuffles. It was accepted as normal in footy. There were nasty incidents – I saw players king hit – but I came to learn the real art lay in intimidation and bluff. There was no need for intentional body blows when the threat of brutality was enough. Go after the ball with a shoulder dropped and nostrils flared, and opponents were far more likely to get out of your way.

Another appeal of controlled violence was the satisfaction I got from sticking up for my friends. If a teammate got into a stoush, I helped him out. Bonds were formed in the tumult. Later, in the change room, we'd laugh about how it all happened. And boast. 'We lost the game but who won the fight? We did.' All that bullshit. Importantly, there were no consequences for the odd fracas in sport, only benefits. At the time, it gave me what I needed: a reputation as someone who could 'look after himself'. Mind you, I never thought this made me special. Most Seaford boys acted like I did. Our first rule of fighting was hit first and hit hard. It was the tribe's motto.

But standing on the steps of The Grand that night, I was scared. I hoped no one would look up and see me there gnawing my nails.

Slugger threw the first punch. He had to rise up on his toes to do it. His left fist swung slow and steady as the second hand on a clock. When it struck twelve, it was on. The strangers who had come for a fight rounded on Slugger. Steve and his mates jumped in after them. The brawl took up the entire footpath. There was kicking, smashing, tumbling and lunging – like a bar-room scene from an old Western movie, but more vicious.

I searched for Steve in the chaos. He was shaping up to one of the strangers. Gone was the timid, softly spoken boy I'd known growing up. At nineteen, he was a strong man, like our father. He threw a flurry of straight rights at a man of similar size; his opponent was going back at him, using both hands imprecisely as his mates joined in. Suddenly Steve was outnumbered. The sight tripped some kind of alarm inside me. A kill switch overrode my nerves, triggering a surge of cold fury. I went wild. This wasn't courage; it was some other primeval reaction. Something animalistic. He was my brother. I bounded one stride down three steps and launched at Steve's attackers. Then I blacked out.

When I regained my senses, as if my wiring was somehow repaired, I was pinning a stranger to the ground. He was trying to get up but I wasn't letting him wriggle free. In my peripheral vision a pair of scuffed brown boots were approaching along the footpath, stopping and starting, waiting for an opportunity. I knew what they were up to. I'd never had someone try to kick me in the head before, but I'd seen it done to others outside The Grand. I raised my forearm to deflect the blow. The kicker had put so much effort into his swing that he lost balance and landed beside me. I leapt to my feet, thrashing my arms like the cartoon Tassie Devil, trying to give the impression I was insane. This bought me time and space to look around for Steve and the other Seaford boys, if they were still standing. The brawl was as frantic as before, although more spread out. Some young men were being dragged onto the empty highway, some were backing away down the footpath, some were lashing out with fists, boots, knees and elbows. Our opponents weren't tiring; their resentment was rising. A couple of them had smashed the tops off stubbies and were brandishing them like sabres.

'They're gunna try and stab us,' someone called out.

It was time to retreat.

I hurried into Uncle Vic's fish and chip shop. My body ached but I was too charged with adrenaline to pause and work out exactly why. Steve made it inside a second or two after me. Our marauding enemies were taunting us from just outside the front door.

'You're trapped,' one of them said. 'We're gunna kill you when ya come out.'

They didn't dare come inside. Uncle Vic's nephews were holding the knives that they used to shave rotisserie meat for kebabs. The nephews told us to go out the back door, which led to a side street off the highway. We said okay and went back into the uncertain night, to hide among the overflowing bins and fossicking gulls.

'We sure about this?' I whispered. 'They could be waiting for us.'

The alley was short. It led to a side street, which had me worried that the enemy had seen us go and ducked around the corner to follow through with their threat. A moment before they had a chance to spot us, we got lucky. A cab came to our rescue. We saw the headlights first, then the smiling faces of two of Steve's friends in the back seat – they had fled the fight early in search of a taxi.

'Fuckin' ripper,' Steve said.

We piled in and told the driver to floor it, straight past the baying mob. Beside me in the back seat, Slugger was bleeding. A piece of glass was stuck in his skull. We should have taken him to the hospital, but he was making jokes about losing one of his Andrew Bews (shoes) so we laughed along and tried to forget about his serious injury. He soon closed his eyes.

Steve turned to look at me from the front seat. 'You okay?'

I could no longer ignore the throbbing pain in my hand. It must have shown on my face.

'Yeah,' I said, 'except for this.' My knuckle was relocated halfway up my fist. I must have hit someone. Maybe someone hit me back. I couldn't work it out. The part of my brain that shut down never restored the images. I was pretty sure I never actually lost consciousness during the fight. I'd just been out of my mind.

Steve looked worried but I reassured him I was fine. I wanted to show him that his little brother could take anything; I was fit for this new manhood, for good or ill. He knew better, but smiled anyway. We were both relieved to be going home.

A day later I went to the doctor to get my hand plastered. Steve got in trouble from Mum for letting me get into a pub fight. She never said anything to me. I didn't know why.

The big brawl didn't put me off the pub scene. The summery nights still saw me drinking and partying. But by day, with a plaster cast keeping me off the beach, I kept my footy dreams alive with a new, improved fitness regime. I took to jogging like never before: twice a day, mornings and afternoons, in preparation for the footy season. I got faster, lighter and stronger. I always ran topless, soaking up the sun. I'd never sweated so much in all my life. I felt like I was being cleansed. All I needed to work out was my running gear, my Walkman and my favourite mix tape. With the right song playing in my headphones, I'd lengthen and quicken my stride to the beat. I became durable, with stamina to burn.

One morning I ran so well that I bounded over entire squares of footpath. I was flying. I daydreamed I was leading the final stage of the Coolangatta Gold. The country's best Uncle Toby's Ironmen, Guy Andrews and Trevor Hendy, were behind me and closing in, but the finish line – the Emanuel Drive street sign – was in sight. I needed one last push. Getting me there was Steve Winwood, singing 'Higher Love'.

I surged past the post, waving to the imaginary crowd lining each side of the street. Doubled over in my front yard, I took gulps of water from the garden hose. The grass beneath my feet became the turf of the MCG. I pictured myself in front of a packed stadium, on this hallowed ground where the first ever game of Australian football was played, back in 1858. I'd researched 'The G' for school assignments. I'd read the description of that first game in Melbourne's *Morning Herald*: 'Most jubilant were the cheers that rang among the gum trees and the she-oaks.' I'd watched my heroes play footy and cricket there. I'd sat beside the enormous scoreboard for the 1990 Grand Final. In my mind the siren had gone. The fans in the grandstands were chanting my name. With my new run-all-day fitness, I could do anything.

3

Under the Pergola

At recess on that first day back at school, I went looking for my mates. Outside the canteen, dozens of kids were queuing for snack food – doughnuts, Sunnyboys, bags of chips. Already, the lunch ladies were hard at work. The courtyard smelled of pies in the warmer. After the long summer holiday, this was about as exciting as it got. It was like opening day at the Melbourne Show, without the roller coasters rattling overhead.

I had three inseparable school friends at Patterson River Secondary College: Adam, Leigh Mackay and Myles Maddock, whose nickname was Doc. Doc was smiling and pointing at me. 'PK! Woohoo.'

'Here he is,' Leigh said, smirking at my plastered hand. 'Iron Mike.'

The boys were lounging on a table beside a barbecue, under the shade of a freshly built pergola. We shook hands. They already knew about my helmet fine, but they were up for another round of laughs at my expense.

'You are a dickhead,' Adam said.

'I know.' I was keen to change the subject. 'Hey Doc, you've grown.'

'Thanks man, yeah I'm stoked,' Doc said. 'Been a big summer.'

We didn't see much of Doc outside school. As the only surfer among us, he spent much of his life chasing waves. He must've grown four or five inches since last year. Doc had wavy blond hair and a smile the girls adored. He was also an artist; the best teenage illustrator I ever saw. Sometimes in class he invented cartoon characters. I was amazed anyone could have so much talent. Doc was always animated: slapping you on the back, punching your arm, throwing his head back in hysterics or protest. Today he had extra pep. We were in Year 12. We were kings of the school.

'So, where's our common room?' he was saying, waving his hands. 'We're seniors now. We need a hangout.'

'Yeah, our own personal, customised rat's nest,' I said, quoting *The Wonder Years*, our all-time favourite show.

For as long as we knew, Year 12 pupils were allocated a room for studying and socialising. We'd heard stories about these big kids smoking and doing whatever else they liked without being bothered by teachers. We'd been looking forward to it since we started coming here as wet-behind-the-ears twelve-year-olds.

'No common room this year,' Leigh told us. 'They've fucked us over.'

Leigh Mackay gave the impression he was laidback, almost flyblown, but he was also unusually intelligent, with a smoke-dry wit and a sharp ear for schoolyard gossip. He hadn't grown taller over summer, but he was broader across the shoulders, and he looked like he needed a good shave. Strong, handsome and athletic, he had everything going for him, including an anti-establishment streak that I admired.

'Who's fucked us over?' I said.

'Those pricks.' He pointed in the direction of the staffroom.

'Why haven't we got a room?' Adam said. 'That's the only thing I was looking forward to.' I could picture Adam playing music all day in the common room; our in-house DJ.

'Blame last year's Year 12 students,' Leigh said. 'They trashed their room. Kicked walls in, left rubbish everywhere. I heard the teachers found a bong.'

'Well, if we can't have our own space, let's take over this one,' Doc said.

From that day on we commandeered the pergola. Built in honour of the former principal, Mr EK Pyers, it came with a plaque that read: 'EK's BBQ'. Using a permanent marker and an offcut from the woodwork room, I soon changed it to 'PK's BBQ'. It would stay that way for the rest of the year.

Our meeting place was at least central. Almost everyone had to pass through to go from here to there. It was perfect for perving at girls – one of our top three favourite hobbies (the others being talking about famous sportspeople and planning for the weekend).

'Rootable?' one of us would say. And he'd point out a girl or say her name.

'Shit yeah,' one or two would respond.

'Aw, I dunno,' another might add.

'Hell, yeah,' Doc would say.

We habitually used the word 'rooting'. Our other words for having sex were chopping, laying, ploughing or slamming. Older boys passed down these terms of aggression. We didn't think twice about adopting them as our own.

After status of rootability, the next question we considered was whether or not an identified girl was a virgin. I understood this was wrong, because we didn't do it within earshot of anyone else. I knew my mother and sisters would have been appalled. But I told myself we were complimenting the girls by giving them our attention. I hoped the girls talked about us the same way.

In reality, I had no idea what I was talking about. Adam was the only non-virgin in our group. I assumed he'd had sex with Emma. But he'd also had a one-nighter with another school friend at a party. This set him apart from the rest of us, even the all-popular Doc, who found it as difficult to express affection towards girls as I did. We were left to tease each other about our inexperience, and tell wanking jokes. There were a lot of those.

I'd been coming to terms with myself for about five years. It all started with the lingerie section in Target catalogues that came to our house free in the letterbox.

I had learnt about sex from the two most popular books of our time: *Where Did I Come From?* and *What's Happening to Me?* I liked their no-nonsense language ('Little people are made by big people…') and silly illustrations. Although, the cartoon on page six puzzled me. There was a naked middle-aged couple in a bath. The wife was sitting, the husband standing, his tackle on display. For some reason he was playing with a tugboat. The caption read: 'Put Mum and Dad in the bath together, and you'll notice something.' Nudity wasn't a revelation to me. My mother and father used to tiptoe starkers from our shower to their bedroom every night (not together), while we were watching *Neighbours* or *Sale of the Century* on the box in the lounge.

The other stories in the books were easy enough to follow: from the fastest swimming sperm I'd grow to be all pimply and hairy. Having learnt the facts of life (except for the significance of the tugboat), I could push on with becoming a man – or, at least, what I thought a man was.

'Seen Louise yet?' Adam said to me on that first day under the pergola.

'Nah.'

I was planning to avoid her for a week or two, until I was sure I was over her.

Louise had transferred to our school in Year 11. I knew my crush on her was serious when I started getting nervous in her presence. I liked the way her hair swayed across her shoulders when she walked, like she was in a shampoo commercial. My assumption was that all the other boys felt the same way about her, but they didn't.

'She's not that hot,' Adam had said.

That made me like her more. I could see something in her others were missing. On the few occasions I talked to her in the schoolyard and at parties, I went to water. Most unnerving was the way she looked at me as if she knew what I was thinking.

She approached me one night at a mutual friend's house. We were in the backyard. 'When are you gunna kiss me?' she asked. Thankfully, I was drunk and self-assured, so I leaned in without a word. After that, we kissed each other at parties every other week. I always made sure I'd had a few beers for composure. One night, she came around to Adam's house and we shared a spa. I still remember the sound of the filter pump humming away in the fern garden. It was one of the first times I'd kissed any girl sober, and it showed me what I'd been missing out on. I rode my bike around to her house a couple of times to watch TV, always looking forward to our goodnight kiss on the front porch. We never went into her bedroom. It never occurred to me to ask her to sleep with me. Sex was something different in my mind, more conquest than love. I didn't connect it with what I felt for Louise.

Another night, she phoned me to talk.

'What's up?' I said. 'We just saw each other. You forget something?'

'I just wanted to see if you got home safe.'

'Righto.'

'And I didn't want to go to bed without hearing your voice again.'

I wondered whether we were becoming a proper couple.

We weren't. It didn't go beyond that. I was hopeless at telling Louise how I felt about her. We never talked at school because I feared people would make fun of me. I didn't know how to be a boyfriend. In the end, she rang me up (I used the second phone in Mum and Dad's room for extra privacy) and said she didn't want me to come around to her place anymore – something about not being able to communicate.

'Okay, whatever you reckon,' I said. The conversation made my chest hurt.

Next day, she called to say she'd changed her mind. I rode my bike like a maniac to her house and we had one last innocent night hanging out. We sat on separate couches in her living room. She patted the seat next to her. I knew she wanted to cuddle. But her mum was in the next room. 'I'm okay over here,' I said. I should've gone and sat as close as possible. Later in the night, we spent half an hour kissing goodbye. Heaven. But that was it. Neither of us phoned the other. I kept pretending to ignore her at school. It was a ridiculous way to behave but I didn't know how to be considerate or loving in public. Maybe she got sick of that. More likely, she didn't feel for me the same way I felt about her. I believed deep down that was the truth.

Adam could see I felt sad about it, now that we were back at school. 'You never know,' he offered. 'You and Lou might hook up again this year.'

'I don't care about her that much,' I lied. 'And I heard she's got a new fella.'

'Yeah, I heard that too. Sorry.'

'I've gotta stop listening to that bloody Wendy Matthews song,' I said. 'The Day You Went Away' was on *Video Hits* on Sunday mornings. I taped it and listened to it over and over, thinking about Louise. I'd actually started to get used to missing her, and I liked it.

'You're a weirdo.'

That was about as deep as we got in our discussions of heartbreak. There was no way I could let myself be seen as vulnerable, even by Adam.

For years, I'd built my life around competition and ambition; feelings didn't come into it. But lately I'd been wondering if there might be something wrong with that. I wrote about it in my diary, but I was incapable of correcting it. Worse, I made fun of other boys if they betrayed feelings of tenderness – just to make myself feel better. Any boy who spent too much time with his girlfriend was a 'soft cock' or a fag.

The school bell rang. One of the canteen ladies pulled down the roller door to close up shop. Doc and Leigh went to class. Adam and I watched younger kids disappear from the courtyard into buildings and portables. We slowly picked up our bags.

'What've we got?' Adam asked.

'Lit,' I said, trying to hide my delight.

4

Mrs Mac

English Literature had taken me by surprise a year earlier. I felt like I'd landed in a unique environment, something like higher learning. Our teacher was Mrs McMahon, but we called her Mrs Mac and she didn't seem to mind. She was youngish (maybe early thirties; it's hard for kids to tell the ages of adults), with dark curly hair and soft eyes. As far as anyone knew, she was the first English teacher to offer a literature class at the school. It was considered a niche subject.

To get the first class going in Year 11, Mrs Mac had needed at least ten kids. In the end, she managed to find twelve: ten girls, plus Adam and me. Adam had zero interest in books. He did it to keep me company, and because he couldn't think of anything else to study as a fifth subject. The girl-to-boy ratio might have helped too.

A year later, Adam and I had signed up again without hesitation. We were a bit late to our first class, a habit built up over six years of sauntering the hallways.

'Just find a seat,' Mrs Mac said. 'And get out your novel.'

She never wasted time or padded out her lessons. We got straight into it.

Our book was *Tess of the d'Urbervilles*, by Thomas Hardy. We were expected to have read it by now, and I'd had a good go at it. I hadn't finished it, but I knew enough to get by in a discussion.

'Can't wait to get into this little beauty,' Adam said, thumbing the pages of his paperback copy. I was certain he hadn't read a page of it. The year before, he'd made it through two entire semesters without reading any of the texts.

'Pleased to hear it, Adam,' Mrs Mac said. She tolerated his sarcasm because it was inoffensive and self-deprecating.

Mrs Mac had already explained that Hardy was a writer with working-class roots who liked to stick it up the Victorian establishment for its hypocritical social rules. I liked that about the author. His writing was impressive in a way I couldn't articulate. But I struggled to understand his 100-year-old language. I'd read the book with a dictionary handy, translating when I got lost.

He was inexorable [unstoppable]*, and she sat still, and d'Urberville gave her the kiss of mastery. No sooner had he done so than she flushed with shame, took out her handkerchief, and wiped the spot on her cheek that had been touched by his lips. His ardour* [passion] *was nettled* [irritated] *at the sight, for the act on her part had been unconsciously done.*

'You are mighty sensitive for a cottage girl,' said the young man.

'Okay,' Mrs Mac said. 'So, what did we all think about this passage?'

I strained to think of an answer that might be considered insightful. Mrs Mac was tilting her head in anticipation of an answer. This was my fourth year with her. When she started as my English teacher in middle school, I didn't care for any learning, but she got me writing stories and I enjoyed them. I wanted to impress her, and kept at it because I could never quite do so. 'I don't quite know what to say Paul,' was one of her summaries of my work. 'You're capable of much more than this.' Then she'd give me almost-compliments, like 'this was a well sustained effort'. I had made a special effort during our class's examination of *To Kill a Mockingbird.* This earned me rare praise. 'You display a sound grasp of the novel and of essay-writing skills. You've come through yet again.' That felt like a breakthrough. She then assigned us to review the movie *Field of Dreams.* This was a home run, and common ground for us, as it turned out. I liked sport and nostalgia. She loved Kevin Costner. 'Thought you might like it,' she said. It felt like a bond had formed.

Before Mrs Mac, my record as a student had been inconsistent at best. Most of the time I was restless: overbearing but compliant. In the schoolyard, I was worse. I didn't think of myself as a bully when I was young. But I can see it now. When I was seven, I started getting in trouble for it. The principal, Mrs Haining, gave me a letter to take home to Mum: 'I feel I should write to you to let you know of the problems we are having with Paul's behaviour. We have been aware since the beginning of this school year of rough bullying behaviour of three boys. We have spoken to them on several occasions but we are still receiving complaints about them teasing and bullying other children.'

It was true. I called timid, thoughtful boys 'wusses' and 'girls'. I had physical advantages at that age and I thought it made me superior. Mrs Haining's letter opened Mum's eyes. She was horrified. I got the 'treat others the way you want be treated' speech. It made sense but took a long time to sink in.

One time, I saw a girl arriving at school and decided to give her a scare for no good reason except that I liked her and had no idea how to show it. Her name was Sam Rowe. I got some other kids to stand along the path near the entrance. We waited till Sam was close before roaring at her. She ran away crying.

It was Adam who helped me overcome this mean streak. He didn't like bullying and always let me know it.

My mother had to handle the fallout from my behaviour because Dad, a truck driver, worked until late in the afternoons. It tested Mum's nerves. A few times, the school asked her to help the staff sort me out. One teacher broke down and cried, begging for Mum to intervene. 'I've got no problems with him at home,' Mum said. She promised to support the school in whatever it wanted to do with me. 'But I'm not going to punish him twice.'

Each complaint about me was different, each complainant working a different angle. One teacher, whose flat, ugly face I'll never forget, actually told Mum that he wanted to go back to the old days in dealing with students like me. He shoved his fist into his open hand, miming a slow punch. My mother almost jumped out of her seat. The teacher cowered inside his sports jacket. 'Let me tell you,' Mum said, 'I've seen what violence can do to children and it's never acceptable. What you're suggesting is disgraceful.' Watching Mum take on this fool made me tearful. I hated that I placed her in that situation but, at the same time, I loved watching her stand up for me. The teacher apologised. Mum and I drove home in silence. She was tiring of this song and dance.

I was the only one of my siblings who created such frequent drama. Jo was the other extravert in our family; she'd given our parents some heartache a few years earlier but later settled down and thrived (she was now in university). Steve and Kate were never any trouble at all.

For some teachers I was an angel. My Grade 4 teacher, Mr Langley (a kind and passionate man whom I adored), wrote on my report: 'Paul spoils his good work with his "offhand" attitude at times. He has great leadership qualities also, but must make sure he uses these properly, and not influence others the wrong way. When Paul is "with you" there is no better student.'

I was 'with' my English Lit class, but I didn't always have the answers. Luckily, I had students like Jane Prentice to show me the way. Jane grew up in our housing estate. Her parents, Marilyn and Len, were well-known locals. Mr Prentice was nicknamed Twinkle Toes for his dancing at local footy club functions. Jane had been a top-of-the-class student since we were six years old. While I was arguing with teachers or being a pest or bully, Jane remained diligent, unflappable. I envied her.

It was Jane who responded to Mrs Mac's question. She was appalled by the hypocrisy of the male characters in Thomas Hardy's book. Some of the other girls joined in. Adam and I could see where this was going.

Mrs Mac pointed out that Hardy was exploring society's reaction to the young, unmarried Tess losing her virginity to an older man. 'He's attacking the notion that the loss of chastity means the loss of purity.'

Mrs Mac turned to Adam and me. 'Let's get a male perspective,' she said.

I fumbled for a moment before plunging in. 'Well, for starters, the cops should've arrested the bloke,' I said. 'Tess was only sixteen.'

Mrs Mac was unimpressed. She tilted her head even further, waiting for my real answer.

'Well, basically the whole town thinks she's a slut,' I said. 'And it's not fair.'

'Yes, but there's more to it,' Mrs Mac said. 'We're talking about Hardy's approach.'

I could feel my face heating up. Being examined on this double standard embarrassed me. In the schoolyard, among mates, it went unremarked. A century after Hardy levelled his accusations against Victorians, I was guilty of the same charge. I judged girls. All the boys I knew did the same. Now, among my female classmates, I was being challenged to explain why. As uncomfortable as it was, I knew they were right to put me on the spot.

Mrs Mac was waiting for me to go on.

The good teachers always demanded more effort from me. My primary school PE teacher, Mr Clarke, used to run beside me in the hundred metres race. One year, I was way out in front of the other boys, but Mr Clarke wanted me to go faster. He screamed at me, his long legs taking two strides to my one. 'This is *slow*, you can go faster, try harder!' I gritted my teeth and tried to beat *him*.

Mrs Mac's use of silence was no less effective.

'Well, he's sticking up for her,' I said.

'He's doing more than that,' Mrs Mac said.

The discussion turned to modern men's attitudes towards women.

'We still want girls to be pure if we're gunna go out with them,' Adam said. 'If they've been with someone else, we might wanna sleep with them but maybe not go out with 'em. That's what some guys think.'

'That's not right,' Jane Prentice said. She'd probably read *Tess* twice and understood all its metaphors. 'A hundred years after he wrote this book, and nothing's changed?'

'It's not our fault,' I said. 'We're not all like that.'

'Oh, come on, Paul,' Jane said. 'What about if a boy sleeps around? How is it different?'

'There's nothing wrong with a girl who sleeps around,' I said.

'But there is, according to your social norms,' Mrs Mac said. 'Adam just said you guys wouldn't want a girlfriend with too much experience.'

I got the feeling Hardy would have enjoyed watching us boys squirm.

Toward the end of the lesson, Mrs Mac asked for observations about Hardy's use of language. I couldn't hold back.

'There was one paragraph I had to read three times because it was so good,' I said.

'Read it out if you like.'

I went slowly, careful not to make a mistake.

'"Perfect, he, as a lover, might have called them off-hand. But no – they were not perfect. And it was the touch of the imperfect upon the would-be perfect that gave the sweetness, because it was that which gave the humanity."'

Mrs Mac asked why I liked it so much.

I knew why but I didn't dare say it aloud. Those words struck me as so honest it made my blood rush. Did I love it because Hardy saw the world the same way I saw it? Was it possible I was romantic?

'Dunno,' I said. 'It's just nice.'

At the end of the class, Mrs Mac asked me to stay behind for a second. To my surprise, she gave me another book. It had a picture on the cover of a patchy sunset over a forest.

'*I Heard the Owl Call My Name?*' I said. 'Is it homework?'

'No,' she said. 'It's not on the curriculum but I think you'll like it. It's a really beautiful book. Something you wouldn't necessarily choose for yourself.'

'Thanks,' I said. 'I'll give it a go.'

I tucked the book into my bag. It was thin, no larger than a birthday card. I didn't know its value, its power to change my life. I was still a reluctant reader. The only novel I'd read for enjoyment was *The Hobbit*. I liked being guided through school texts by Mrs Mac. But the occasional thrill I got from a sentence or paragraph passed quickly. Once or twice, I contemplated reading more widely. But then I reminded myself I was no bookworm. I was an athlete.

5

The Shrink

Back when I was nine, my parents asked me if I wanted to sit for a private-school scholarship. I liked tests, so I said yes. I wasn't sure why they asked me; my older siblings hadn't taken the test and they were always more conscientious than I was. I guessed it was because I was having trouble controlling my emotions in the classroom. I did okay on the exam, well enough to get offered a half-scholarship, but I told Mum I didn't want to change schools. 'I wouldn't know anyone,' I told her. Mum said fair enough and didn't bring it up again. I knew my parents couldn't afford to pay any school fees. They might have been more insistent if I'd won a full scholarship. But I didn't, so there was no use wondering.

When I was twelve – and still blowing up a lot during sport and classes – I was sent to a psychologist, at the school's suggestion. Everyone said I was too intense. I could lose the plot in the middle of any competition, big or small. The worst incident was at an athletics carnival. Some kid from another school beat me in the one hundred metres sprint and I pretended he'd only won because I hurt my ankle near the finish line. Tears pooled inside me before bursting up and out through every hole in my face. I couldn't stop crying. The shame of losing control in front of so many people made it worse. A concerned teacher told me to calm down and I told him to fuck off. Mum was watching on, mortified. When she tried to step in, I told her to leave me alone.

'Show some respect to your mother,' the father of a friend said. 'Stop faking and take responsibility for your actions. There's nothing wrong with second place.'

He was right. I said sorry, but he told me he didn't want to hear it.

On the drive home, Mum threatened to give me away to a boys' home.

At the shrink's office, I was led into a small room while Mum and Dad waited outside. They were given some reading material – photocopies of pages from an American psychology journal. The headline was 'Chronic Frustration'. I found the photocopies later and read with interest that I had some sort of condition that needed to be overcome by parental, scholastic and psychiatric intervention. 'Goal: The student will learn to calmly accept situations that are not within his or her control.'

The shrink, in a tone as flat as the bay at dusk, wanted to know why I threw tantrums. 'Why are you so emotional do you think?'

'Dunno.'

'What makes you frustrated?'

'Dunno.'

'We're going to try something today,' he said. 'Some people call it hypnosis, but I like to call it relaxation.'

I may well have scoffed. Hypnosis sounded to me like some sort of voodoo. I regarded it as silly, impotent magic that would only work on the weak-minded. I expected him to bring out a swinging watch, like they did on the telly, and I was disappointed when he didn't use this as part of his act. He told me to imagine I was in my favourite place in the world. Could be a beach with blue water. Could be a football field. Could be anywhere I wanted.

'Just listen to me, nothing else,' the shrink said. 'Breathe in through the nose, out through the mouth, Paul. In and out.'

I closed my eyes to make him think I was complying. I concentrated on where I was in reality: not far from the Frankston pictures. I thought about how my friends and I had seen a movie there not long ago, and cheered and hooted through the kissing scenes.

'Have you found your favourite place?' the shrink said.

I'd forgotten he was there.

'Now that you're relaxed,' he said, 'I want you to think about your toes, just your toes, and I want you to wiggle them.' He did the same wiggle-and-relax trick for the rest of me, all the way up to my head. I played along for a while, before realising I was slipping into sleep. I told myself off. He almost got me. Soon I was heading home in the back seat of our family's Toyota Hi-Ace van.

'Feel better?' Mum said. 'What was it like?'

'Did you get much out of it?' Dad said.

'Nah, not really,' I said. 'Was a bit of a joke. Do I have to go back?'

'Yes.'

At the second session I found myself listening more intently to the shrink's friendly voice. 'Imagine your favourite place in the world,' he said again. 'But I don't want you to imagine you're playing anything. No games. No competition. I just want you to go to a nice place and sit there. Breathe in, breathe out.' Then he started up with the toes again. I thought about a tropical beach.

For some reason I was a little boy again, about four years old. I was sitting on a blue and red Lilo, looking down into the crystal-clear water.

'Look around you,' the shrink said. 'You're safe in this place. Breathe in, breathe out.'

My shoulders felt hot from the sun. Somehow, I was older now, almost a teenager. I was standing in the water up to my thighs. I was thinking about chasing the shadows of fish below me. Next thing, the shrink was clicking his fingers to wake me up.

My body was so heavy it felt like part of the chair. I felt a wonderful nothingness. No urgency. No self-consciousness.

'How long was I out?' I said. I didn't want to move in case the luxurious feeling went away.

'Not long,' the shrink said. 'Just remember that place. You can go there whenever you feel like you're a bit out of control.'

And I did. Having been shown how to reach that quiet place, I put it to good use.

I breathed in, I breathed out. I became less volatile. I felt like the shrink had tamed me. It was only when I got a taste for grog years later that I felt that control slipping away.

6

Thinking About Drinking

Though I was a seasoned drinker at seventeen, it felt like it was only yesterday that I'd been telling my folks, with utter sincerity, that I would never touch alcohol.

'That's good, mate,' Mum had said.

'You don't believe me?'

'No, but we'll see.'

As a young teen, I'd been inspired to make my lifelong teetotaller pledge after hearing legendary football coach Tom Hafey talk about his temperance. Unusually for a man of his era, he drank not a sip of alcohol. Instead, he had chosen a life of fitness. He did hundreds of push-ups and sit-ups every day, and sipped tea. If it was good enough for the brawny Hafey, who looked thirty years younger than he was, it was good enough for me.

I didn't lack for other role models in this regard. Mum hardly drank. Dad usually stuck to light beer. I suspected he'd been a binger like me as a young man but, like smoking, he gave it up when his children started to look up to him. I reckoned it helped that our oldies weren't dinner party types. We never had adults over to get on the sauce and clink glasses and spill wine on the carpet. Once or twice, I saw this type of looseness at other houses.

Some parents hit the bottle hard. But we never stayed long enough to see how those nights ended. My friends had stories of being bundled into car seats or spare rooms so the grown-ups could keep socialising. I didn't know whether to be jealous or relieved. I envied the free spirit of parents who partied harder than ours, but I understood how lucky I was to be raised in a household of consistency and peace.

With peer pressure bearing down on my good intentions, I'd started to wonder if dodging the drink might make me boring. At fifteen, I downed my first beer in preparation for an underage disco. It was part of a six-pack I shared with Adam and Leigh. We drank it on the banks of Kananook Creek so no one would see us.

'Now I know why they call it piss,' Leigh said.

I knew what he meant. The beer was warm and hard to swallow. But it gave me a dreamy sensation. 'I feel fuckin' great,' I said.

I strode into that disco no longer afraid of being out of place. I stared at girls and started to believe they were staring back at me. I felt cool. I danced and didn't care what I looked like. Adam, Leigh and I laughed all night.

At sixteen, I'd been part of a government health campaign to help curb under-age drinking. Ah, the irony. One of my uncles, Tony, who was an artist, wrote and illustrated a booklet for the campaign called *Thinking About Drinking*. He used Adam and me as models for his drawings. When it came time to launch the campaign, Tony asked us to come along. We were the token teenagers, the booklets' target audience. An ABC TV news crew interviewed me. I was completely underdressed in baggy shorts, T-shirt and sneakers without socks. The journalist, a young woman, asked me how peer pressure contributed to the culture of binge drinking. I told her it didn't. I said kids could make their own choices in the suburbs 'where we live'. In my best outer suburban drawl, I told the world: 'If you say "No, not drinkin' tonight," no one cares.' Adam backed me up with matching certainty. It was what we thought the reporter wanted to hear. And it was what we wanted to be the truth. What I wanted to tell the reporter was that we were the wrong people to ask. I hadn't even been blind drunk yet. I was also too naive to understand how peer pressure worked. It wasn't something you could see; it was a feeling, a directional flow, like a pulse. It was happening to you before you knew it.

The first time I'd got really drunk, I was at home. I had to see what it was like. With Mum and Dad away for the weekend, Jo and her boyfriend had bought me a dozen VBs. Jo told me not to drink too much. I suppose she thought I would try a can or two with a mate. I didn't tell her my plan was to down the lot, alone, while watching the movie *Dead Poets Society* on our second TV in the back room. Eight tinnies down, while breaking the seal, I vomited – a whole-body eruption of warm lager, Savoy bickies and French onion dip. Most of it landed in the toilet.

Next time I got properly pissed was at the pub with the boys. After a few tries, we did it regularly.

7

Racing Quadzilla

My routine after school had always been to avoid study. Final year was no exception. On school nights, I'd boot the footy at a lonely light tower across the road from our house. There were no power lines in our 1970s-built estate. The wires were buried underground. Instead, we had iron-shafted light poles, like oversized lamps, rising out of the nature strip. I used one of them for target practice.

When we were younger, Steve and I spent hundreds of hours out on the road kicking a ball to each other. Most of the time we employed drop punts, making the ball spin backwards on a straight line. For variety we tried torpedoes, sliding the ball off the side of our sneakers to make the ball spin smoothly around a pointed tip. A well-executed torp was a beautiful creation; I got so good at them I could make them curve and dip and fly like paper planes.

These days my brother was off doing his own thing, so the light post took his place. I tried to hit it from twenty metres away, then forty, fifty. When I was successful it would make a clanging noise and I would pump my fist and wave to my imaginary crowd. After each kick, I walked to pick up the ball, and bounced it all the way back to my next launching point. My favourite kicking spot was on the nature strip outside the front fence Dad had built around our yard. From there, the post was due west. During the long twilights of February, I had to squint to see the pole against the glow of the sinking orange sun. All that time, I was daydreaming about the coming season.

The hold that football had over me was powerful. It was how I imagined church people felt to have supreme faith. Was that why I heard commentators call Australian football a religion? Natural or supernatural, it didn't matter. As the new season loomed, I thought about the game constantly. Everything else was a distraction. I couldn't wait for the matches to start so I could wear my boots. The sound of a football team jogging in studded soles on a concrete floor, running out the players' race, like the sound of a hundred playful hammers tapping away at once, gave me goosebumps. Playing. Watching. Imagining. The green oval was my shimmering ocean before I knew what the sea looked like.

I was trying out for a representative football team called the Southern Stingrays. It was part of a new Under 18s competition set up by the Australian Football League to prepare teenagers for the big time. The AFL was only three years old, having rebranded itself after almost a hundred years as the Victorian Football League. Sport was turning professional all round the world and I wanted to play games for a living. If I could pass the audition and become a Stingray, I'd be able to spend the rest of the year competing in stadiums around Melbourne against the best teenagers in the state under the scrutiny of recruiters from AFL clubs – one step from glory.

I got my plaster cast cut off just in time for the Southern Stingrays weekend-long camp – the last audition – in beachside Somers, south of Frankston.

Our squad was whittled to about fifty young players. The club had been cutting the list since before Christmas. One more cut loomed. The Stingrays could field players from an enormous region, stretching from Beaconsfield in the east to Sorrento, the southernmost tip of Port Phillip. Most of us were seventeen but there were a few sixteen-year-olds. A handful had already turned eighteen. Some of the players were automatic selections. A few of them had played for the Stingrays during the previous inaugural season. I felt my place in the squad was tenuous. I'd been in other representative teams growing up, but I was always unspectacular at this higher level. My best traits – balance, decision making, composure – were subtle. There were a lot of players my size who could play my favoured position in the backline. If I were to make the final cut, I needed to distinguish myself in the eyes of the head coach Greg Hutchison. At this point, I doubted 'Hutchy' even knew my name.

A pre-season camp like this was a combination of emotional bonding and physical torture. If you could put up with the pain of being pushed beyond your limits, it could be the loveliest escape from regular life.

Some coaches treated these getaways like military programs, acting out their private fantasies of becoming drill sergeants. I didn't mind that concept. I could play soldier for a while. I particularly liked the teamwork involved in completing physical tasks. Before Christmas, on our first of two camps, we ran as a squad up Arthurs Seat, a small mountain near Dromana on the other side of the peninsula. It was the hardest thing I'd ever done. Near the summit, I rolled my ankle and almost fell off the track into the sharp grass. I collapsed, moaning in agony. Sweat stung my eyes. My limbs felt heavy as stone. I wanted to give up.

'Don't stop,' someone said. I looked up to see the face of a boy called Kristian Leilnors. Everyone called him Scratcha. I never found out why. He was one of the leading players, gregarious, good-looking and popular. He looked just as tired as I felt but he wasn't stopping. 'Keep going,' he said. 'You can fuckin' do it.' He patted me on the back. His simple encouragement worked like an injection of fuel. It got me back on my feet. That's how it works. That's the good stuff among boys like us. Little words and gestures here and there. You pass them on. You get them back. You feel looked after. With the urgings of Scratcha, a boy I barely knew to say g'day to, my mind cleared. We made it to the top together.

This final camp at Somers was even tougher than the mountain climb. On Saturday, we trained to exhaustion. Some boys vomited from the efforts they made just to keep up with the schedule of tasks, most of which involved running. Early the next day, our fitness coach, Andrew Crouch, took us on a coastal road run. 'Crouchy' took the lead. We fell in behind him, like a mob of brumbies, up and down hills overlooking the brightest blue Westernport Bay. Crouchy was a long-legged athlete in his late twenties – skinny but strong. His running style reminded me of marathon runner Steve Moneghetti. Crouchy was in such good shape he barely sweated, and he was rarely out of breath. I'd become fond of his booming voice and repetitive instructions. 'Keep up at the back, don't drop off. Don't drop off!'

By midmorning, as the sun had found its full strength, we were still running. My entire, aching body was dripping wet. I tried to stay close to the front in the hope Crouchy might notice me. A desperate search for recognition churned in my brittle marrow.

My devotion to competition was natural. I needed it. Most of my life I'd had a gut feeling that time was running out. It made me uneasy. Football stopped the clock, let me live unhurried, flowing.

While I ran, I studied the others, measuring myself against their shape and form. The squad boasted some impressive athletes, none better than a quietly confident kid called Shayne Smith. 'Smithy' was statuesque, with long blond hair and tan skin. His full frame would've caught the eye of passers-by on any beach in the world. He had that all-Australian golden lustre, a bit like a taller Grant Kenny. Arguably the best teenage footballer in the nation, he'd kicked sixty goals in the same competition last year. It was a surprise to everyone he wasn't drafted straight into the AFL. Apparently, some clubs went close to picking him up but baulked at the last minute. They had questions about his potential to improve as an adult. Was he already as big as he was going to get? Could he get any quicker? Was his kicking at a high enough standard? I thought they were silly questions. From what I'd seen at training, Smithy was a star. He was the only player in the team others held in awe. Even Crouchy seemed to treat him with reverence. I couldn't wait to play alongside him – if I made the cut. Jesus, if only I could make it.

Crouchy quickened his pace. 'Find another gear boys if you can, let's push it.' The frontrunners in the group went with him. I kept up, barely; trying to fill my lungs with rushed gulps of salt air; wiping my drenched eyebrows with the back of my hand.

I was driven by the fear of dropping off the pace, missing out. It was an obsession I'd had for as long as I could remember. In Mum's box of photo albums there was a baby picture of me with an oval-shaped ball. Another one shows me running around on my first birthday at my grandmother's house, with a footy under one arm of my knitted golden jumper. I always loved the feel of footies. I used to take them to bed as if they were teddy bears. In my waking hours, I found it impossible to walk past any kind of ball without picking it up and playing with it. It was a compulsion; as natural to me as breathing. If I couldn't find a football, I'd roll up some socks and make a game. Steve and I played matches at night inside the loungeroom or along the hall. We kept going until we broke something, or Mum and Dad told us for the umpteenth time to stop thumping the walls.

I loved other games too. On my seventh birthday my parents gave me a pair of cricket pads with shiny new buckles, and some flash gloves. I wore them all day and all night. It was the middle of football season, however, so I was also wearing a long-sleeve black and white Collingwood jumper. I've never boasted a better outfit or bigger smile. That same year Dad started taking Steve and me to watch Collingwood games on Saturday afternoons. We went to stadiums closest to home: Waverley Park (previously VFL Park, then AFL Park), and Moorabbin (St Kilda's home ground). If we were lucky, we'd head all the way into the city for a game at the MCG. Steve and I hero-worshipped particular Magpies. We stayed awake in our bunk bed, listing all the players at Collingwood in order of their jumper numbers. Our favourite wore thirty-five: Peter Daicos. On the back of the black duffle coat he wore to games, Steve had 'Daicos' in white letters. When he outgrew the coat, it became mine. I loved Peter Daicos as if he were part of our family – the way he sidestepped and ran in short bursts, the way he could kick a ball and make it spin this way or that, how he took marks on his fingertips. Commentators said he did the impossible. In fact, he was showing a boy like me what was possible, if I trained hard enough. If I pushed myself to new limits.

'There's the water,' Crouchy said, as we neared the beach. 'We'll stop when we get to the sand.'

I heard some groaning from those boys struggling at the back. The fitter players were buoyant, pushing us on with their words. 'Work hard, boys. Don't give up.'

Hutchy was waiting on the sand, smiling at the sight of us. The coach clapped to get everyone's attention. He'd organised a series of activities to finish off the weekend. 'We're calling it the Stingrays Olympics,' he said. 'Let's have some fun with it.'

Hutchy had played for Melbourne in the VFL. Neat, clean cut, mid-thirties, he seemed a warm, generous and patient man. But it was still pre-season, so I hadn't seen him under pressure. I felt myself craving his approval, in the same way I did with my father, hoping he would make eye contact with me when he spoke to the team.

Split into two groups, we spent the next couple of hours competing in a variety of events. Last of the day was the fifty-metre dash. Only the fastest kids from each team entered. I'd won beach flags a few minutes earlier, so I put my hand up to have a go. Not that I had much hope of winning. There was another boy in the race who was a national-level runner. He was the clear favourite. He wore his hair in a ponytail and had enormous leg muscles. Someone reckoned his nickname should be 'Quadzilla'.

Hutchy drew a finish line in the sand near the water's edge. The other boys crowded round the coach, who surprised me by saying: 'I'm tipping an upset – I reckon Kennedy'll win.'

'No way,' the others shouted.

Quadzilla and I trudged up the beach to the start line. I composed myself by imagining I was on a football field and we were about to chase after a ball. I told myself that my advantages were my short legs and chunky bum – perfect for the soft sand track. Speed was a big part of my love for footy. I'd always wanted to go fast. I got my first real chance when I was five, when Mum got a part-time job at Roller City, the local skating rink in Seaford. She managed payroll, cleaned the toilets, sold tickets and oversaw the discoes, including celebrity appearances. At closing time, after we'd helped stack the skates back into their racks, Mum would let Jo, Steve, Kate and I take to the rink, which was painted bright blue and shone like a lake. I would start off cruising in a zigzag pattern, hands behind my back, peacocking. At first, I had to clomp around in rental skates. Then I got Steve's hand-me-down speed skates. They were black with a yellow racing stripe. Crouched low, face scrunched in effort, I would pump my legs as fast as they would go, thighs burning. My crowd was roaring but I couldn't see them. The world was a blur.

Hutchy put his whistle to his mouth. I leaned forward, dug my toes in. I felt as strong and light as a kite. Hearing the shrill whistle, I took off, buffeting my hairless chest against the breeze. A few of the boys watching on later told me that when I hit top speed my face screwed up, and I appeared deranged. They laughed, although I thought they were cheering.

The race must have lasted all of six seconds. I dived at the finish and won by a nose.

'Told yas,' Hutchy said. I was spitting out sand at his feet. He looked at me and nodded. That was when I knew I was going to be a Stingray.

Often I think about that race on the beach; returning to my younger body, and feeling the heat, power and daring. I was flailing, not gliding. But I was sure I was going to make it.

8

The Pier

The beach had always been a big part of my life. But in 1993, even that was looking shaky. The Seaford pier, a favourite haunt for young and old, had been earmarked for demolition by local authorities, while feisty locals were fighting to save it. These older residents remembered the pier as a mainstay in what was essentially an old fishing town. They saw it as a part of history. We kids saw it as the perfect launching pad for sun-kissed fun.

But come late summer, reporters and bylaws officers were making a big deal about how deadly the pier might become. After countless days of jumping into the water, everyone was suddenly being told it was illegal to hurl ourselves off the tall pylons. Signs were erected to say leapers would be fined. 'Injury warning as divers defy peril,' barked the lead story in the *Frankston Standard*. Sandbanks that shifted with the tide were part of the problem. The newspaper recalled nasty accidents in the 1980s, when four people were left quadriplegics and nine others were taken to hospital with spinal injuries. A front page carried photos of kids diving off the end of the pier into the shallow bay. Two boys were dangling off one of the new warning signs, giving the photographer the bird.

There was a time-honoured pecking order of jumpers at our pier, with splash-size a significant determinant. Bigger was always better. We mainly did laybacks and horsies. The most skilful among us could produce a kerplunk that sent water back over the crowd, standing four metres above. That was something I aspired to. Adam was better than me at executing laybacks. His splash was socially acceptable, without raising eyebrows. In comparison, I was useless. My timing in laying back as I hit the water was always off, either too early or late. People laughed at my attempts. Instead of persisting, I chose to go with a third option: diving.

Balancing on the top railing, I leapt over the small lower jetty attached to the pier. I imagined I was Johnny Weissmuller taking flight in the old Tarzan movies on Sunday afternoons. The water was only about two metres deep. I was lucky not to break my neck. It's a boyhood truth that some of us were prepared to risk death or paralysis to avoid the shame of not making a splash. But I have to admit it was thrilling, if not joyful, to test my skill against chance. It was fun being so high in the air. On entry, the water was cool and silent. Ignoring the dangers, I decided to dive again and again, as often as I could, before summer ran out.

At the end of those February days, when long twilights began to fade, the moon rose early to watch the sun go down, and the colours of the horizon – streaks of orange, red, purple, silver and aquamarine – drew people from their homes. I took the time to watch the sunsets, the most beautiful I'd ever know. Then I'd climb the rails again and leap one more time into the calm below.

9

Moving Shadow

Three or four times a year, storm clouds as big as mountain ranges gathered on the western side of the bay. Dark as bruises, they came charging at us from across the water, sparking lightning flares as they went. In other parts of the world people knew about earthquakes, cyclones or bushfires. We only knew about these storms, and what we needed to do in the twenty minutes before they hit: close the windows; bring in the dogs; put the car in the garage; turn the trampoline upside down; get cosy; and listen for the sound of the first hail to hit the rooftiles.

It was under the cover of one of these thunderstorms that the killer, no longer satisfied with carving up kittens, hit the streets. He wore a green jacket, blue cap and black sneakers with burnt soles to disguise his tread. He carried with him a handmade knife and fake gun. He'd made the weapons on the sly in the factory where he worked, in an industrial estate two blocks from our family home.

He'd been shadowing girls and young women along our streets for three of four years; trailing from a distance. But this time would be different.

It was a Friday. A storm was coming to test us all. The summer nights were long gone. The autumn chill had given way to bitter blasts of winter. Darkness now fell like ash clouds each evening. The sky rumbled, cracked, groaned and burst open. In the downpour, a bus was travelling from Frankston to Langwarrin. 'Langy', as we called it, was a gumtree suburb sprawling inland. The bus driver would later tell police the rain was so heavy outside he didn't pay attention to passengers coming and going. With windscreen wipers on full, his concentration was on the road. The route went out past the cemetery, over the freeway, beyond the historic homestead and a shopping centre.

Sitting on the bus was Elizabeth Stevens. She was eighteen. Elizabeth had been studying an English TAFE assignment at the library. The ride home was only ten minutes, maybe fifteen in this weather. Elizabeth wouldn't have been looking forward to the dash from the bus stop to the front door of her home. It wasn't a long way, but still, she'd get drenched. At least her uncle and aunt, with whom she lived, would have the house warm and her dinner waiting.

Elizabeth pulled the cord to alert the driver to her stop. He squeezed the brake. The door exhaled and opened. No words were spoken. She stepped into the rain.

The teenager left the main road, heading home down a side street. Out of the gloom a hand clamped over her mouth. He threatened to kill her if she screamed. He said he had a gun and was prepared to use it. Grabbing Elizabeth's hand, he led her into Langwarrin's Lloyd Park, a vast reserve of sports grounds and bushland.

Elizabeth never made it home. Alarms were raised that night. A local man found her body on a dirt track the next morning.

Branches covered her torso, but the killer had made no real effort to hide his crime. Homicide detectives arrived to examine her. She had been strangled and stabbed. The storm had washed away forensic evidence. Police urged anyone with information to contact them. Who saw Elizabeth on the bus, getting off the bus, walking home? No one came forward with helpful information.

The murder shocked us all. For the first time in my life, I read stories on the front page of the newspapers before going to the sports sections. One of the *Frankston Standard* headlines read 'Hunt for killer'. It ran with a picture of a mannequin the cops had dressed to look like Elizabeth Stevens. They'd tied it to a street sign outside a shopping strip in Long Street, Langwarrin. We were supposed to take note of what the mannequin was wearing (Reebok runners, grey tracksuit pants and a loose-fitting blue windcheater), but I was haunted by the doll's straight-ahead stare. I came to think of it as Elizabeth herself.

Elizabeth Stevens was a name we all came to know. The paper reported on her funeral; only sixty people attended, which I thought was too few. It turned out she had moved from Tasmania only about six months earlier. She didn't know many people. The funeral celebrant told mourners: 'She loved children, she was young at heart, she had a wonderful sense of humour, often dry witted. No one can harm her now. She is safe and in peace.'

Smaller headlines told us police had no suspects: 'Much effort, but no clues for officers.' Police turned to handing out leaflets at Frankston train station. They wanted to speak to the driver of a white four-wheel-drive seen near the football ground the day after Elizabeth went missing. Some people suggested that the police were having more success tracking the murderer than they were letting on; they were keeping the breaks in the case to themselves. 'They'll arrest someone soon, you watch.' I hoped it was true.

I heard adults question whether Elizabeth Stevens's murder might be related to other sinister disappearances. Three years earlier, twenty-three-year-old Sarah MacDiarmid had gone missing from Seaford. She was last seen at Kananook railway station (between Seaford and Frankston). Her car was found in the car park. It was locked. But forensic police found red smears inside. There was a bloody puddle under some bushes not far away. A search of the area turned up Sarah's cigarette lighter, but nothing else. No one had seen Sarah go to her car but police took a witness statement from a couple who'd heard a woman scream and say, 'Give me back my keys.' Investigators assumed Sarah was murdered but couldn't say for sure. Where was her body? Did she actually die at the scene? Many years later, well-known Detective Charlie Bezzina wrote in his book, *The Job*: 'Sarah had no enemies, so it was clearly a random, opportunistic attack by strangers. It seemed she just happened to be in the wrong place at the wrong time.' He believed there was more than one abductor. By 1993, a reward of $75,000 was being offered for information that might lead to an arrest.

In 1991, a pair of policemen had actually come to our door. They were hunting another killer. A six-year-old girl called Sheree Beasley had been abducted while riding her bike to the local milk bar in Rosebud, forty minutes south of Seaford. Her disappearance had made national news, as did the discovery of her body in a drain three months later. She'd been raped. At the time of her disappearance, witnesses reported seeing a girl crying in the back of a stranger's car. The driver had grey hair. A computer image of the suspect was released to the public. Someone saw it and phoned police, telling officers the computer image looked like Dad. At our front door, the police explained that someone had seen him driving his truck and reckoned he looked like the photofit of the killer of Sheree Beasley.

'Who said that?' Dad asked.

'Someone who saw you driving in the area.'

'Yeah, who?' Dad was not easily shaken, but this riled him.

'We can't tell you that.'

They wanted to know where he was during the abduction. Dad shook off his annoyance and produced his truck logbook. He kept a record of every job he ever did. In his fine sloping script, he was able to show them where he was when Sheree Beasley was abducted. They thanked him but needed more proof. Mum later went with Dad to the Frankston police station to back up his story. Dad was further put out. He held two things dearest: his family and his integrity. He'd been spending his adult life building them.

I was angry that anyone could have questioned my gentle father's character. But I supposed, at a glance, he could look imposing. Thick across the shoulders and chest, he maintained neatly parted hair, like a greying Superman without the curl, and a black moustache. On his caveman-club forearms were small tales of his past: two do-it-yourself tattoos from his brief time in the navy. My eyes were always drawn to his large arms, brown as well-oiled timber. When I was a little tacker, I would grip his bicep, whereupon he'd hoist me like a crane, and let me hang, whole body giggling, until I couldn't hold on any longer. 'Dad, you're so strong,' I would say, after he put me down and I was sure I wasn't going to wet myself. Yet when I cuddled into him on the couch, he was softer than my favourite blanky with silk edges.

Dad was a man of contrasts, which is not to say he was mysterious. A truckie with a poet's penmanship and a lover of old books, he considered equally the plight of all living creatures. He was fond, if not obsessed, with the loveliness of birdsong. Not satisfied with our backyard species of magpies and mynahs, he built an aviary and filled it with budgies and quails. Typical of all his handiwork, the cage was well built – five metres squared, two metres high, with pot plants, nesting boxes and hollowed logs.

Dad loved listening to our new residents. Their conversation and music soothed him. The older he got the more he seemed to celebrate the simpler pleasures of life.

Perhaps Dad was preparing for his children to one day leave the nest. My older siblings were already young adults. After years as a gang of four, we were going our separate ways. My older sister Jo had been our ringleader from day one. She was tall, outspoken and cool. I wanted to be like Jo. Steve and Kate were the quieter pair of our gang, yet they were also happy-go-lucky. Steve was particularly handsome. He had angelic blue eyes with long, curved lashes that made grown women envious. He was also industrious, careful. From a young age he could concentrate on intricate tasks. It meant he could fix things – bikes, fishing reels, anything mechanical. He put me to shame with those abilities, but I didn't hold it against him. Kate was only thirteen months younger than me, but she always felt a lot younger. She was my baby sister. Little Katie. Steve called her 'youngster'. We had always made it our job to protect her. When she got hit with a cricket bat in a schoolyard accident one day, I went wild and attacked the boy who did it.

It wasn't his fault, but my sister was crying, and someone had to pay. Kate bounced back quickly. She had the best way of laughing, a rising cackle that was highly contagious and sent me silly no matter where we were.

Jo was busy studying in the city at William Angliss College (hospitality and business), and working part-time at as a bartender at the local Returned Services League. Four times a year she worked for Frankston Council as a leader of its school holiday programs. She had turned twenty-one in February. We threw her a party at a local hall. Jo spent any spare time she had with her boyfriend, Ashley, a likeable full-forward from Seaford Football Club.

Steve was also a footballer with Seaford FC. He'd become a dashing, skilful backman and a leader of the team no less, always in the paper as one of the best players. A full-time worker from the age of sixteen, Steve had left school to be an apprentice plumber. He was now in his final year of training with the Gas & Fuel Corporation. Steve was also in love, spending more and more time at his girlfriend's house. For the full seventeen years of my life, my big brother had never been further than shouting distance from me. Now we hardly made time to speak to each other during the week.

That left Kate as the last one in the nest with me. The last to make it through childhood, anyway. We'd always been close. I still tried to look out for her in the playground, not that she needed (or wanted) me to. She was shy, and I suspect I embarrassed her with my grandstanding and bluster.

10

'Give it Your Best'

———————

I'd only ever experienced selection disappointment once in my short footballing life. I was used to making the team.

But one night, when I was ten, the unthinkable happened. At the time, Dad was my coach in the Seaford Under 11s. My brother and I were in our bunk beds. Steve was asleep. I was awake, fantasising about winning the Brownlow Medal. Mum and Dad were talking in the kitchen about an interleague football carnival that was coming up. They must have thought I was asleep, otherwise they would have been whispering. My parents rarely fought in front of their children; it was a rule of theirs to settle arguments in private. There was tension, if not angst, in their voices.

'You should've picked Paul,' Mum said.

'I can't do it,' Dad replied. It was his role to select one of his players to represent our team in a Frankston representative side at the carnival. 'I have to choose another boy.'

'But Paul's the best player you've got,' Mum said.

'I agree, but I'm not going to do it,' Dad said.

My mother kept urging him to change his mind. Go Mum! But for once, she couldn't budge him.

'My decision's been made.'

I started to cry into my pillow. It meant the world to me to play at a higher level, to show everyone I was special. Dad came into my room, sat on the edge of my bed, ran his hand through my hair.

'Mate, I've picked someone else to play in the interleague game,' he said. That boy was my friend Andre, a likeable and determined back-pocket. 'I would've liked to nominate you, mate, but Andre might not get another go at it and you'll have plenty more chances to show everyone what you're made of.'

'Okay, Dad,' I said, wiping tears from cheeks.

'There's always next year, Paul,' he said. 'Thanks for understanding.'

He wasn't apologising, he was explaining. For a long time, I thought Dad had made that decision to avoid accusations of favouritism. Maybe so, but he was also doing it out of generosity. He had a soft spot for all-heart competitors like Andre.

Dad's two-year stint as my coach was full of those lessons. We lost a grand final under his stewardship, and skipped off the field delighted that we'd done what he asked us to do. 'Just give it your best, try your hardest,' he always said. 'And you'll be satisfied at the end of the game, no matter what the score is.'

Dad's caring nature lived long in the memories of those other boys, many of them underdogs, or 'battlers' as he fondly called them. Later in their teenage years my old teammates would go out of their way to stop Dad – they called him Mr Kennedy – in the street to thank him. No man had ever treated those boys with such respect, particularly the ones without father figures in their lives.

He knew how they felt. He had lost his own father when he was eleven.

It was March 1959. He'd spent an afternoon helping his father,

Jack, paint the family's back fence. Jack said he was 'feeling crook' and went into the house to rest. The boy stayed in the backyard. He heard a thud but didn't think much of it. When he went inside later, he found his father on the floor, having fallen off the couch. It was a fatal heart attack. Jack was forty-four.

There was grim commotion when all the other adults came to the house. 'I got pushed aside,' Dad recalled. He wasn't allowed to go to the funeral. Why do we underestimate our children?

'Do you miss your dad?' I once asked.

I knew it was a silly question, but I was trying to find out as much as I could about my father, and he never seemed to mind my curiosity.

'Oh yeah,' he said. 'Even now, I might be doing something for the first time and I don't know what I'm doing and I wish I had someone to show me. I've been that way most of my life. I wish he was around to show me what to do. Especially, when I was your age. That was when I was a bit lost.'

I felt both guilty and grateful to not know how he felt. He was always close to me. I never had to go searching for him or wonder what it would be like without him.

Mum once told me Dad felt bad about not being able to save Jack's life. If only he had gone inside the house sooner. If only he had found him straight away and shouted for help. This type of regret was too much for me to handle so I tried to forget she'd told me that.

After losing his father, Dad grew up quickly. The family lived in suburban Belmore, in Sydney's south-west, a few cut out passes from Belmore Oval, home of rugby league team Canterbury-Bankstown. Dad remembered going to school at Belmore North Primary, playing cricket and marbles, lapping up the ritual of 'milk issue' every day at recess. An unenthusiastic student, he was happiest on holidays. He had always loved helping out in his father's backyard workshop, where Jack had had a small business weaving chairs and tables, a smoke always parting his lips.

Like Mum, Dad was born into a family of eight. A World War II veteran of campaigns in Egypt and New Guinea, Jack had been a clerk with a medical unit. 'Like Clinger in M.A.S.H.,' Dad explained. 'Without the dresses.' In old photos, Jack Kennedy is tanned, tall and lion-strong, with a flashy smile.

The family had no income when Jack died, so the old workshop was turned into a bedroom and let to boarders. Legacy helped my grieving grandmother, Eileen, buy her children school uniforms and books. Whenever we were at Safeway in Seaford, Dad would see a Legacy collector and make a beeline to give him a couple of bob.

'Legacy were good to us,' he would say each time he told me about his childhood, looking at me to make sure I appreciated the hardship, and the helping hands that got the family through the worst of it.

Dad's first job was delivering newspapers, *Daily Mirror* and *The Sun*. He told me he enjoyed his paper round so much it didn't seem like work; the major attraction was meeting three or four other paperboys from different routes at a nearby milk bar after knocking off. If he worked weekends, he'd earn up to three pound a week. He spent some of his money on pinball machines. He gave the rest to his mum.

After leaving school, he started an apprenticeship as a fitter and machinist with NSW Railways. He liked hanging out with other apprentices but didn't care for the work, so he tossed it in and tried other ways to earn a buck: fitter's assistant on a silo construction project, labouring for a local builder (turned out to be cleaning bricks – he lasted three days), factory job (two weeks) and labourer at Roselands Shopping Centre – to pay off the monthly instalments on a loan for his first car, an FE Holden.

Dad often told me he regretted his lack of direction through this period of his life, but I never saw him wallow. 'You have to get experience somehow,' he would say.

I was always desperate to find out about Dad's sporting history. He told me he started playing soccer when he was ten. It was his first team sport. He used to ride his bike, his tenth birthday present, to home games. Dad said Jack never watched. He hoped his father might be more interested in seeing him play rugby league, but that chance never came.

He wouldn't tell me too much about his social life as a teenager in Sydney, but I knew he was a big weekend drinker. He told me he didn't like the smell or taste of beer when he first had a go at it, but soon discovered it could boost his self-confidence. I knew the feeling.

11

The First Game

Dad stuck his head through my sliding bedroom door on the morning of my first Stingrays game.

'Nervous, son?'

I was lacing up my new black-leather dress shoes. I'd already got dressed in my black slacks, a polo shirt and my Southern Stingrays nylon jacket – black, red and yellow.

'Yeah, a bit.'

Mum leaned in.

'Very spiffy,' she said.

By the time I packed my bag, Mum and Dad were waiting for me in the Hi-Ace. I climbed in the back.

'Beautiful weather for footy, mate,' Dad said.

It was a typical April morning, crisp and bright.

'Bloody oath.'

'How exciting,' Mum said. She was as toey as I was. Match days were her favourite too. 'Get a good sleep?'

'Yeah.'

I always slept soundly before games. Nerves usually came midmorning.

Mum and Dad wanted to chat to me on the drive to the

stadium, but I didn't. I put on my headphones and pressed play on my Walkman. By 1993, most kids had Discmans but I loved my Walkman, and I trusted cassette tapes not to jump like CDs. All the way to the ground I listened to 'Walking in Memphis' by Marc Cohn. A contemplative country pop tune, it wasn't your typical pre-game rev-up. But it had somehow got into my blood. Play, rewind, play, rewind. The piano got me going. I started rocking back and forth in my seat. It was a habit of mine to bite down on my mouthguard all the way to matches, breathing through my nose, imagining how I might perform when the first quarter started. It was my meditation.

As a junior player I'd never really got tongues wagging. It was only later, in the Seaford Under 17s team, attached to the senior club, that I started to stand out. Within two seasons, I won the Mornington Peninsula league best and fairest medal and got invited to train with the Stingrays. Friends my age were becoming bored of organised sport, as if they'd outgrown its childishness. Not me. I was being drawn closer to footy year by year. By now I understood the game, its unique patterns and rhythm. I knew it like it knew me.

To outsiders, Australian football looks shambolic, but it has its own way of flowing. I pictured it as a rollicking river with eddies and currents; if you paddled along the same waterway for many years, you'd come to understand its movements, as well as its anomalies. Even the oddly shaped ball became more predictable as it bounced this way or that or went twisting in the air. These were the nuances that couldn't be learnt quickly. Footballers called it reading the play. I could read the play, though at this new representative level it wasn't an exceptional gift. Everyone else could read it too.

We arrived at the stadium, Moorabbin Oval. Dad drove into the car park and stopped behind the main grandstand. I saw him talking to me, so I took off my headphones.

'What position are ya playing?'

'Centre-half-back.'

'Ah, good.' Dad knew it was my favourite spot in any team. I first played there when he was coaching me seven years earlier.

'Thanks for the lift,' I said, swinging my bag over my shoulder.

'Good luck, love,' Mum said. 'Go get 'em.'

Up until the previous year, Moorabbin Oval hosted AFL matches. It had been St Kilda Football Club's home since 1965. The stands were run-down but the field was immaculate, like a golf course fairway. I'd first played here for the St Kilda Little League team when I was ten. Little League matches used to be played across the entire field at halftime of VFL matches. Wearing number eleven to emulate Saints hardman Greg Burns, I kicked two goals. The crowd cheered each time. I looked for Mum and Dad in the stand behind the goal but there were too many people for me to find them. A few weeks later I played a Little League finals game at Waverley Park and won a bike for being best on ground. I never saw the prize. Mum gave the bike away to one of my cousins. 'You've already got a good bike,' she said. 'Do you mind?' My siblings suggested our community-minded mother might be going too far with this fairness-for-all approach. I couldn't have cared less. Playing Little League was reward enough. And she was right. I already had a good bike.

I was also familiar with Moorabbin Oval as a spectator. Dad was a St Kilda barracker; he'd taken Steve and me to plenty of Saints matches over the years. I was in awe of players like Lockett,

Burns, Trevor Barker, Danny Frawley and Nicky Winmar. But my sentimental favourite was Robert Harvey. He was my hero because he came from Seaford. I used to see him running around the streets of our housing estate, soaked in sweat but barely puffing. A mere sighting would create conversation around our suburb. 'I saw Bob Harvey running! Did you see him too?' Harvey was our Halley's comet.

Now, Moorabbin Oval was off Broadway. AFL executives were striking the suburban venues off their schedule as part of a stupid 'ground rationalisation' policy, which only made sport less accessible to people in the outer suburbs. It was lucky for me, however, because the stadium was going to be the Stingrays' home ground for the entire season.

I walked out onto the oval to greet my teammates, athletic working middle-class kids like me, white skinned but with suntans that gave them a collective glow. All were wearing our slacks and leather shoes uniform. Most were shuffling around with hands in pockets.

'Here he is,' said our skipper Ben Delarue. 'How are ya, PK?'

'Yeah, good, you?'

'Couldn't be better.'

Benny was six foot, and squarely built, as if he were bred to play football. His family was from Upper Beaconsfield near the Dandenong Ranges. He had a country-boy appearance and reputation; he was easy going, with a warmth and contentedness that gave others comfort. But he wasn't anywhere near as affable during matches. In our practice games, he'd revealed himself to be our most aggressive teammate. He accelerated into collisions, like a car with no brakes. Yet he was also highly skilled. There were no weaknesses in his game, or none I could see. Like me, Benny was a backman. I was happy we'd be so close to each other. When Hutchy named him captain during the week the whole team agreed it was a smart move.

'Can't wait to get stuck into this mob,' Benny said. He was holding a shiny red football, sliding it across his palms and fingers as if to massage them. He passed the ball to me and I did the same, revelling in the leathery caress of a pristine Sherrin.

Other teammates said hello and shook hands. We made small talk. In a representative team like this it took time to get to know each other. There were no other kids from Seaford. I felt oddly insecure. I knew I'd find other friends. But it was taking longer than I'd hoped. During the summer months I'd tried to make friends within the squad. One afternoon I had thought I'd made a connection with a boy called Aussie Jones. We kicked a ball back and forth and talked for ages. I liked him a lot. A couple of weeks later he got cut. Someone said the selectors reckoned he was too small. It turned out he was a year younger than me. (He would return the following year, get drafted by St Kilda, and became an All-Australian.)

Out on the wing, our opponents for the day, Central Dragons, had formed their own well-dressed huddle. Home teams always got the centre square in these pre-game gatherings.

Benny asked me if I knew about Central's coach. 'His name's Ray Jordan,' he said. 'They call him Slug.'

'Used to be a commentator, didn't he?' I said, recognising the name from the 1980s Army Reserve Cup matches on TV. He was in the commentary box the day Collingwood player John Bourke tripped an umpire. Jordan famously said, 'I think you've gotta take the boy off.' I didn't know at the time but old Slug was also a former state cricketer and celebrated Under 19s and reserves coach in the VFL.

'He's bloody mad,' Benny said.

'How d'ya mean?'

'You'll see. You'll hear him during the game.'

The competition we were about to begin playing in – the Victorian State Football League – had a lot of household names attached to it and it was attracting plenty of publicity. Selected teams were printed in the *Herald Sun*, Melbourne's number one tabloid newspaper. This excited me more than I was prepared to let on. I'd never had my name in anything other than the local paper. There were ten teams: Southern District Stingrays, Eastern Ranges, Western Jets, Northern Knights, Central Dragons, Geelong Falcons, Bendigo Pioneers, Ballarat Rebels, Gippsland Power and Murray Bushrangers. The star players from the previous year's inaugural season had been catapulted into the AFL. An athletic redhead called Justin Leppitsch had been drafted to the Brisbane Bears from the Southern Stingrays. I wanted to follow in Leppitsch's footsteps. We all did.

'Time to get changed, fellas,' Crouchy said. Our summer-camp fitness chief was now coach Hutchy's match-day runner. His job was to organise us before the game and during breaks, as well as running Hutchy's messages out onto the ground during the four quarters.

I savoured this hour leading up to a game. It was a reflective period of promise. The concrete change room room smelled like massage oil and old sweat. I liked the odour almost as much as the feeling of butterflies in my stomach. I also enjoyed watching my mates twitching with the same tension I felt, while getting massaged and strapped. Some boys paced and listened to music, trying to ignore everyone else, nodding their heads to the beat of grunge or heavy metal drums, flexing their jaws, steeling themselves for what lay ahead, trying to ward off performance anxiety. We all knew we were about to be judged by AFL scouts, among others. I didn't feel I had to worry about that. I was just grateful to be playing. My focus was on earning the respect of Hutchy, Crouchy and my teammates. I wanted to show them that I was worthy of being in their company. This gave me an edge. Self-consciousness had never been part of my game, not at Seaford when I was growing up and not now; in other parts of my life, yes, but not here. When I ran onto the oval my aim was simple: to hurt the opposition with hard tackling, protect my teammates with body and voice, show courage, and win the ball in contests. I did this happily, without ego – even if my face was comically scrunched up in effort. I was luckier still that this approach to the game let me enjoy every beat of the pre-game crescendo.

I changed quickly into my shorts, socks and boots, saving until last the pleasure of pulling on my guernsey. Our collared jumper was yellow with a brown Stingray chest emblem. The Stingray looked angry and intimidating, we hoped. I wore thirty-six on my back. Once I was in uniform, I went to a trainer and had my hand taped. The broken bone had entirely healed but a doctor had recommended I play with some padding. It looked like I had another cast on, but I could still mark the ball when needed.

Then I got into some handball drills with others who were ready. Handballing is an underrated skill in footy. Everyone talks about kicking, but speed of hand is just as critical. An excellent handballer has three outstanding qualities: fast hands (to avoid being tackled the moment you win the ball); sharp eyes (clear vision, including peripheral, to see teammates who then become your targets); and ambidexterity (no use being a gunslinger with one pistol when you could brandish two). I could shoot handballs from either hip, a bonus of having broken my right index finger when I was ten and being forced to improve my non-preferred side.

Handballing in the rooms turned into a brief game. Who was the slickest? The answer was Shayne Smith. He was the best at almost everything.

Crouchy went around slapping backs. 'Plenty of touches, boys, not long to go now.'

I took the opportunity to sneak away to the toilet. I had mild diarrhoea before every game of football I ever played. My insides churned with a joyful anticipation. On the way out of the bathroom, I splashed my face with water, winking at others as I went.

Hutchy called us in for a last chat. We gathered close, skin to skin. A shoulder bump here. A tap on the arse there. A clip behind the ears. It felt natural to be so intimate.

Hutchy had a tightness in his expression I hadn't seen all pre-season. 'Remember, it's the first game,' he told us. 'It might take you a little while to settle in. Try and touch the ball as early as you can. Just get your hands on it. Even if it's just rolled out of bounds – go and get it and hand it back to the umpy.'

Greg Hutchison's strength as a coach was the way he catered to the fears and needs of individual players. When he spoke like this, gently and thoughtfully, I felt like he was talking directly to me. 'Get a feel for the ball. Get yourself into the game. That'll settle you down. Go from there. We're in this together, boys.'

Every player was making a noise now. Some were grunting, some were breathing deeply, some were muttering, and a few were shouting encouragement. We were rousing as one. I was shocked to hear my voice above the others.

'C'mon, let's smash 'em,' I yelled. One of my teammates was looking at me. He, too, seemed surprise by my outburst. I smiled at him and he nodded his approval.

'Don't give 'em a fuckin' sniff,' someone else roared.

We hollered about winning, but our war cries weren't driven by a desire for victory. It was an expression of our natures. Boys like me craved the contest; we desired it as we desired love. There was a fire inside us. In our blood. I felt it every day and it was easily fanned. I didn't know who put it there. It had caused me problems, but I was grateful for it. I hoped it would never die.

Hutchy took me aside as we bustled out. 'Nice and physical from you today,' he said. 'Aggressive. Get us going.'

I put my mouthguard in and bit down hard, started shadow boxing.

Hutchy smiled. 'Good luck, boys,' he called as we lined up behind Crouchy in the doorway.

My body relaxed, as it always did at this exact moment. I let my head fall loosely on my neck to one side and then the other. I wriggled my fingers and rose onto my toes. My feet felt strong in my moulded-sole boots, the muscles in my legs taut as trampoline springs. My skin, warm and slick, tingled and tightened. Everything inside me, including my heartbeat, was at ease: all the butterflies were gone. A calmness overcame me. I was as happy as I could be. Life was almost too wonderful to be true. I had come to know and rely on this feeling of elation. It was a bit like how I felt on Christmas mornings years earlier, when Jo, Steve, Kate and I would gather outside the loungeroom door and wait for Mum and Dad to wake up, so we could charge in and open our presents from Santa. 'Go for it, kids!' The magic was in the anticipation.

Only the first game of the year was way better than Christmas.

Crouchy led us out. We moved down the race like riot police about to quell an uprising. There was some indistinguishable shouting above the tap-tap-tapping of our boots on the concrete. Then we stepped onto the grass, Benny first. I had to shield my eyes from the sun before I could take a good look around. The grandstands were empty, save for our families and a few men with clipboards. There were no clouds in the soft blue sky. The oval looked so large as to be borderless. All this space was for us.

'How good?' someone said. The voice belonged to Jeff White, a lean ruckman with square shoulders and a high-jumper's leap. Whitey was only sixteen. He was very skinny, but a best-on-ground performance in a practice match had propelled him into the side ahead of schedule. There was something special about him. He grinned a lot, laughing at even the hint of a teammate's joke. He looked down at me and flashed one of his big-eared smiles. 'Can't beat this, PK.'

Warming up with short sprints, I relished how much energy I had. I wasn't straining for breath. My boots seemed so light that they barely touched the turf.

I liked to think about this game of ours in mathematical terms. To be impressive, I needed to win as many contests as possible. The field was vast – the largest of any ball sport in the world – so the first challenge was to run to as many contests as possible. The more contests I was involved in, the more chances I had of winning the ball. I'd heard a quote from film director Woody Allen that made sense to me: 'Showing up is eighty per cent of life.' So it was with footy. Show up. Be in the action. Give yourself every chance of taking the prize.

The Dragons trooped out of their change rooms in the same military style we used. They were enormous, and muscular. 'C'mon, boys. Here we fuckin' go,' they were shouting. We shouted back at them. 'First fuckin' bounce, boys.' Two tribes going to war. It was a final ritual before the captain's speech.

Tradition says the skipper always gets the last word before the game starts, with his teammates leaning in to listen. I was desperate to hear what Benny would say. Already I'd started to look up to him like an older brother, even though we were the same age. I suspected he'd be a distinguished orator on top of his other talents. After winning the coin toss (we'd be kicking towards the old members' grandstand end), Benny called us in. His eyes bulged and his shoulders flexed. His intensity drew me so close he might've smelled my breath. There was some growling through mouthguards, then we all fell silent.

I'll never forget Benny's spectacularly short speech. 'Let's kick arse.'

That was it. I felt silly for expecting more. But it was perfect.

'YEAH!' we roared, breaking up and running to our starting positions.

I ran to the backline. Benny was nearby. He smiled. We each found an opponent to stand beside, shook hands for good luck. The siren sounded. Time stopped. For the next two hours, life didn't exist beyond the painted white lines of Moorabbin Oval. No thoughts of school, our friends, our families, our futures. Nothing else mattered. It was just us and a ball.

I found the heightened pace of the game easy enough to manage. I anchored myself to my opponent, wary of letting him touch the ball. When I dared, I went searching for kicks. I ran and chased, collided with Dragons. My fellow Stingrays did the same. But it was clear from the start that today, we wouldn't be kicking arse. The Dragons were better, to say the least.

Our centre-half-forward Smithy was waiting to impose himself, but we couldn't get the ball to him. I heard Hutchy calling out from the grandstand, his voice already strained. It was almost quarter time and we still hadn't kicked a goal. The Dragons had bagged several. Crouchy ran all over the ground, urging us to do more, go in harder.

Seconds before the first break, I saw a chance to attack from defence. The ball was on our forward flank, about seventy metres from our goal. I'd followed my opponent all the way down to the edge of the centre square. The Sherrin was mongrel-punted into my path. Instinct told me to get after it. I picked it up, stepped off my right foot and weaved past a lunging Dragon. The pitch of my teammates' voices rose sharply. 'Kick it, kick it.' My problem was I was running to my left, and I was a right footer. My ambidexterity didn't go all the way down to my feet. With no time to straighten, I dropped the ball on my unnatural side. The kick was ugly, but it had enough force behind it to land near the top of the goal square. It bounced through for a goal. I ran back to my position up the other end of the ground, patted and praised all the way. It was our first goal of the year. I'd like to say I meant it.

At the break, Hutchy patted me on the shoulder and said quietly, 'Thanks.'

'No worries,' I said.

He would never know how special he made me feel in that instant.

The rest of the game was a struggle. Jeff White kicked a goal and showed his class with several high marks. Smithy kicked a goal too. Starved of opportunities, he couldn't do much more. The Dragons spent the day demoralising us at the other end of the ground – my end of the ground. They had some brilliant players, whose names I learnt after the game. There was the elegant and powerful Justin Murphy (who would go on to play for four AFL clubs) and the classy full-forward Julian Kirzner (a future key forward at Essendon and North Melbourne). They kicked seven goals between them.

In the third quarter, when the margin was blowing out, I noticed an old man bellowing from the outer wing terraces. Belatedly, I twigged: this was Slug Jordan. At one point I heard him call out my name. 'Stop that bloody Kennedy from running off half back!' It confirmed to me I was having a decent game.

The scores in the newspaper the next day would record a thrashing. Central Dragons 17.17.119 – Southern Stingrays 6.14.50. I was named best player on the losing team. When I saw Dad in the social rooms after the game he said, 'Bad luck about the result, but you did well.'

'Thanks,' I said. I was trying not to beam. I was disappointed by the defeat, but my satisfaction of having proven myself at this level was overwhelming.

'You happy?'

'Yeah, I did all I could,' I said.

'Not every day you get singled out by Slug Jordan,' he said.

12

Mum in Black and White

We hosted the winning Dragons at a post-game function in the social rooms. Coaches made speeches, we ate sandwiches and drank cans of Solo, Fanta and Coke. Hutchy gave me an award, some sort of gift voucher. I was weary but excited. It was still early afternoon, and I had another match to go to. Collingwood was playing Geelong at Victoria Park. Dad dropped Mum and me off at Moorabbin station so we could catch the train to the inner-suburban stadium, which had been home ground of the Woodsmen for one hundred and one years. I still had my Stingrays polo shirt on, hoping to attract a few looks. There goes a prospect!

A capacity crowd of thirty thousand was already there when we arrived. Mum and I found our seats among the season ticket holders in the outer forward pocket. I recognised some of the faces of other regular supporters.

I told myself that next year, I'd be on the field, not in the grandstand.

'Could be you out there one day,' Mum used to say. 'Anything's possible.'

Mum adored the Pies. It was a family love affair. Both her brothers, Geoff and Bob, were Collingwood diehards. Bob actually played for the club as an Under 19 in the early 1960s. I didn't know how deep Mum's affection ran as a barracker until she woke me one morning to tell me that one of our favourite players, Darren Millane, had died in a car crash. She was crying as if he were one of her close friends. Millane was a wild man with a soft heart – Mum's type of hero. She went to his funeral to pay her respects.

'How we gunna go?' she always asked before matches.

I helped settle her nerves with some rational analysis of our chances of seeing a victory. I was hoping Peter Daicos, now in the twilight of his career, would have a day out. He'd retired briefly in the off season, then changed his mind. Thank God. But I knew my idol was getting old. He'd even cut off his mullet, a signature of his youthfulness. I didn't want to believe Daics was past his best, but it was possible.

The home crowd was rowdy and relentless. I understood why visiting teams didn't like playing here. Abuse of opposition players was rife. Some of it was racist. Two weeks later St Kilda champion Nicky Winmar would answer disgraceful taunts by lifting his jumper and pointing to his black chest.

The teams burst through the banners and went to their positions.

'Come on, Daics,' I bellowed.

'Yeah, carna Maggies,' yelled Mum.

The match was a treat to savour. I could hardly believe our luck. Geelong's Gary Ablett, the most exciting player in the league, kicked seven goals. Daics kicked eight. Collingwood won by ten points. The Macedonian Marvel's last goal was a left-foot special – a gift to all who loved him, and a message to those who doubted he could still be great.

The Collingwood three-clap chant went around the ground.

Mum and I sighed and smiled and shuffled out of the ground shoulder-to-shoulder with other barrackers singing the theme song. I wanted to hold on to this moment. How many more weekends would I spend with my mother like this?

The time we spent going to and from matches was just as precious as the football itself. I got to talk to Mum, really talk to her, about our lives: where I was going, where she'd been. I asked questions about her upbringing, looking to see why I was the way I was.

After a while, I knew her story as well as mine.

She was born in Chelsea Hospital in 1947 – a Baby Boomer – and won a cutest bub contest the same year. She had five siblings. Her parents were Grace and Norm Hankinson. Norm died when Mum was twenty-one. He was an affectionate man, who always praised his children. That's why Mum was like that with us.

I often asked Mum about her schooling.

'I was a bit of a rebel,' she told me. 'I left school when I turned fifteen. That was normal back then.'

'Were you smart?'

'I was, but the only subject I liked was sport. I left before they asked me to.'

Mum also told me about her first true love: Elvis Presley. For the first eight or nine years of my life, Mum had me believing she used to date Elvis. I told a lot of people that The King was 'almost my dad'. A fed-up teacher at primary school tried to set me straight. To which I sternly replied, 'How would you know?'

Mum eventually confessed she'd only ever been out with

Elvis in her dreams. I was pleased for Dad. It had been worrying me that he was Mum's second choice.

My mother never failed to light up when she told me about being a young adult. She left home when she was nineteen, after joining the navy. She was posted to Sydney. Her time in the WRANS (Women's Royal Australian Naval Service) turned out to be death-defying.

One night, to celebrate her twentieth birthday, Mum took leave for a catch-up with old school friends, in the border town of Wodonga. She got a lift from a young man who may have been a boyfriend. She never said either way, but she did say he nagged her to wear a seat belt, and we're all glad of that.

It was late and it was raining as they approached a one-lane bridge. Headlights were coming at them. Later, Mum's friend said his brakes had locked up: she remembered screeching, sliding. The crash left them trapped. When an ambulance arrived, medics used tools to cut off the car's roof. Mum's knee was crushed; three of her vertebrae were fractured and her chest was bruised from the belt, which saved her life. She was taken to a nearby hospital, eventually released to spend the next three months at HMAS *Penguin* awaiting knee surgery.

Sometimes Mum showed me the scar on her leg. I could see her replaying the events in her mind. I always knew her to be a nervous passenger, even sitting alongside Dad, who drove cautiously. Often, she'd flinch approaching a sharp corner or a bend in a mountain road. It was difficult to understand her panic because it didn't fit with her otherwise fearless personality.

After recuperating, Mum went back to work. She visited royal agricultural shows along Australia's east coast, enticing young people into the navy, the same way she'd been recruited in Melbourne. After a few events, her boss asked her to drive with him to Brisbane for a show. He was an officer in middle age. Mum said no. Why would she do that when the navy was paying for her to fly? 'C'mon,' he said. 'Where's your sense of adventure?' Again, she declined. Soon after, she was reassigned to an office in Sydney, opposite Garden Island. Here she became a typist for the navy's newspaper. Mum said the editor and sub-editor always had binoculars on the windowsill to search for nude women in nearby apartments.

As her son, these stories embarrassed me. As a man, they still do.

Peeping Toms aside, she adored the Sydney lifestyle. I only knew her as Mum: homemaker, protector, hard worker, mid-week basketballer, barracker of Maggies. But I never had trouble imagining her as a younger woman, heading down to Bondi to bake in the sun, or dancing with friends in the King's Cross nightclubs.

That glorious period of youth between growing up and settling down doesn't last long. I was looking forward to it. I was almost there.

My mother had vulnerabilities like everyone, but she was open about those too. She was always dieting, despite looking forever fit and healthy. (The only soft drink we ever had in the house was Tab, Mum's diet cola.) She had trouble relaxing, particularly in the evening, and was often looking for yoga or meditation classes to attend. She worried about us kids: Kate's and my schooling, Jo and Steve driving at night in their cars. Wet roads made her tense. But above all, she was resilient.

She decided to start playing golf when I was about thirteen; she took lessons and picked up the game easily. One day, while Steve and I were having a round of nine holes with her, Mum got hit in the head by a ball. She bent over in pain. Steve and I had a go at confronting the man who'd hit the ball and failed to call out 'fore'. I was crying. Mum said she needed a minute to compose herself. The ball left a dimpled imprint on her skin, a centimetre from her temple. I saw her grit her teeth. 'Let's keep going, I'll be okay,' she said. We finished the round.

When I was twelve, Mum went back to school and completed a diploma in welfare studies. She called herself a 'mature-age'. One of my favourite photos was of Mum wearing her gold-trim gown at graduation; we framed it on the wall beside her Elvis mirror. She soon became a case manager for Fostercare, placing at-risk kids in new homes. It could be dangerous work. Some dads who lost their children were resentful. Mum got threatened but never talked about quitting. In fact, I'd never known her to be happier.

'Someone has to do the right thing by those kids,' she'd say.

Dad simmered when he heard Mum talking about these abusive men. 'Weak bastards,' he'd say. It was about as close as he came to swearing in front of my mother and sisters.

Dad had joined the navy in 1967. He met Mum at a rugby dance in Sydney soon after. They were lucky, I think. Two of the most loyal, loving and generous people had chanced upon each other.

They went out for two years before Dad proposed. During their engagement, he was posted to the HMAS *Melbourne*. He never served in Vietnam, but on 3 June 1969, while on a training exercise in the South China Sea, the *Melbourne* collided with a destroyer, USS *Frank E. Evans*. Seventy-four American crewmen died. Dad was on duty at the time of the accident. He could hear the screams for help from the drowning sailors, and the terrible silence that followed.

13

Making a Buck

Dad and my uncle Garry Parker were my first men-at-work role models. I watched them building our house together. They didn't swear. They didn't tease. They were kind and respectful. They worked hard but at the same time, they were having fun.

Garry was a local footballer, life-saving champion, son of a war hero, and a carpenter of rare skill. My father had no official trade qualifications, but he could master any tool and make anything he wanted. I remember marvelling at both men climbing up and down walls, holding nails between their teeth, setting up plumb lines, moving quickly without rushing. Garry could hit in a nail with a single blow. He challenged Dad to do the same, just for a laugh; Dad persisted until he could do it too. I liked to sit and watch them eat lunch, making sandwiches disappear in a few bites so they could resume their labours. 'Let's get back into it,' they'd say with full cheeks.

On one of these spring days, Mum got the older kids to ride to the milk bar to buy drinks 'for the thirsty workers'. Garry opened his can of Solo and drank it all without taking a breath. Like the ad said, 'it's light on the fizz so you can slam it down fast.' He burped, said pardon, crushed the empty can under his boot, and gave it back to me. I couldn't wait to do that when I grew up.

In later years, I got a closer look at Dad's work habits when he let me tag along while he drove his truck. He was an owner-driver of a new orange and white three-tonne Mazda with a long, broad tray. He worked for a transport company called TNT. I got to watch him navigate traffic from one side of the city to the other, going from depot to depot, picking up and dropping off blue wooden CHEP pallets loaded with goods. Dad was generally easy-going behind the wheel, although once or twice he seemed peeved at young forklift drivers who took too long to unload his deliveries. I studied his fast hands when he tied ropes to secure his load. The stickman tattoo danced on his forearm when he threaded and looped the ropes. I also paid close attention to the way other men acted towards Dad. It was a relief to see he was respected, even though he didn't act like them, at least not the ones who spat and swore and made comments about the bare-breasted models on the posters of depot walls. My favourite part of those long days was the homework Dad gave me to pass the time. It was usually during the holidays or on curriculum days, but I never minded; I liked schoolwork when Dad gave it to me. He wrote out page after page of maths equations. I raced through them to impress him, getting them all right. 'Done!' He gave me ticks and wrote out more sums, never losing patience, always praising me. He said I was a sponge. When I did art at school, I drew pictures of trucks and cars with TNT on the side, a tribute to his industry. One day Dad confided in me that he sometimes wished he were an interstate truckie, rolling all day and night in a big rig. I agreed. It sounded like the life.

'Maybe I could do that one day.'

'You can if you want,' Dad would say. 'But you might want to do other things when you grow up. Make the most of that brain of yours.' He'd look out at the road and let his words settle on me. 'My advice is to stay in school as long as you can. I left when I was fifteen but you can go all the way through, maybe even go to university.'

I liked the sound of that, too. But I couldn't wait to start working.

By the time I was seventeen, if I wasn't in school or at footy training, I was working part-time at Kentucky Fried Chicken. I had tried out for another job – sorting glass at a recycling centre – but it only lasted a day. My co-workers all looked sad; with a kind of melancholy I suspected might be contagious. I couldn't believe people worked full-time in such a place. I told Mum about how desperately boring it was to sort through coloured glass on a conveyor belt for eight hours. 'That's why you've got to do well at school,' she said.

Work ethic was the cornerstone of both my parents' lives. Where we worked didn't matter. As long as we were applying ourselves to a task and getting a regular wage, they didn't mind what we spent our money on. A lot of the kids I knew had jobs at the newly built McDonald's in Seaford. Macca's was okay but it seemed to me like such a big operation, too many chefs.

Kentucky, as I called it, was a take-away-only joint on the highway. It helped that it was right across from the beach, and that I loved fried chicken.

One night towards the end of my shift, I answered the phone in the Kentucky office. The manager, Craig, heard my voice and rushed in to take the receiver away from me. 'What're you doing in here? Thank you, I'll take it. Who is it?'

I gave him a dumb shrug; I was just the cook.

'I'll put my boss on,' I said to the caller.

My job was to defrost, flour and fry the chicken, heat up the nuggets, make the gravy (yuk) and mash the potatoes (just kidding, we used a packet mix). After closing time, I cleaned the store. It wasn't a bad gig. I ate nuggets whenever I wanted and picked all the crunchy bits off the ribs and legs when no one was looking. The worst part was when people found out I worked there and asked me to identify the secret eleven herbs and spices. I didn't have an answer. On the brighter side, I loved the smell of the store. Someone told me once it was The Colonel's policy to somehow fan the fragrance of the chicken onto the streets to mesmerise passers-by. I believed it.

Craig had a brief conversation with the caller and scribbled down a phone order. 'Okay Sergeant,' he said. 'As long as you're here by ten o'clock to pick it up, that'll be fine.'

He walked out of the office scratching his head under his red visor.

'Can you quickly make a bucket of chicken?' he said. 'I'll make some mash and gravy. It's for the Frankston police.'

'It's gunna be a rush,' I said. 'You should've told them we're closing.'

'Can you just do it?' Craig said.

'No worries. Take it easy.' A few minutes later I had a fresh tray in the warmer, ready for the cops to get. The clock ticked over to ten. We locked the doors, the front desk girls went home, and I scrubbed the floor and changed the oil in the cookers. This part of the role was my secret pleasure. It was really a three-person job to clean the whole kitchen in twenty minutes but I took pride in making sure I did it within the time limit.

When I finished cleaning, I found Craig at his desk, muttering about the police.

'Don't know who they think they are. Should I ring and remind them? No, if they're not here, they're not here.'

At half past ten he conceded they'd forgotten about their order. 'Well, that's what ya get.'

'I'm gunna head off,' I said.

'Thanks for your effort,' Craig said. 'Take the chicken with you. I'll only throw it out otherwise.'

'Righto, might as well.' I took the pieces of chook out of the warmer and filled a bucket to the brim. I stuck the bucket under my arm and rode my bike one-handed to Adam's house. He was waiting for me on the porch, his red curly hair glowing under the doorstep light.

'Was I convincing?' he said. 'I was, wasn't I? I'd make a good cop.'

'Nice job,' I said.

We headed to his backyard to feast on our ill-gotten gains in the spa. Luke the dog kept us company from the sidelines. It felt like a victory feed. The last time I'd been here was the night I spent canoodling with Louise. That seemed like a dream now.

While we filled our faces, Adam and I talked about girls. He told me he'd broken up with Emma. 'I just told her I wanted to spend more time with me mates.'

I was surprised; they seemed happy. I wondered whether it was because of my badgering.

'How'd she take it?'

'Not good,' he said. 'She's not talkin' to me now.'

I didn't know what to say. 'I feel sorry for her.'

'You kept tellin' me to do it.'

'Yeah, but I didn't think you'd listen to me.'

I was selfishly disappointed. Adam and Emma's relationship had been a bonus for me. In the past few months, I'd started to get to know Emma's friends. A bridge had been built between the boys and girls. We'd started spending more time together at school and weekend parties. For the first time I could actually hold a conversation with female students.

'Oh, well it's done now,' Adam said.

I'd like to boast that we ate the entire bucket of Kentucky. But four pieces was my limit, and I felt sick afterwards. The world is full of delicious traps.

14

Dick Togs

I knew our school wasn't fancy compared to a lot of others, but it didn't really sink in until there was a big swimming carnival in the city. Somehow, Adam and I had made it through to this regional competition. We weren't outstanding swimmers. In fact, the only time we were in the water was when we went jumping off Seaford pier. But, apparently we were competent enough to represent our school at a meet at Melbourne's State Swimming Centre. It was also a day off school, so we happily caught the train in.

We'd never heard of the schools we were competing against, but all our rivals were in tracksuit uniforms and looked serious about racing. 'We might be in a bit of trouble here,' Adam said. 'They've all got fuckin' dick togs.'

Adam was wearing Okanui board shorts. I had footy shorts.

'Poofs,' I said about anyone wearing Speedos, although I secretly admired those athletes. They all had broad shoulders, big chests, and stern game faces. I wished I had dick togs. 'Wouldn't wear 'em if you paid me.'

Adam was entered in the backstroke and couldn't swim fifty metres. He had to stop mid-race and throw in a couple of freestyle strokes. I was in the breaststroke and came dead last –

dog-paddling to the wall. We shrugged off our shame and laughed all the way home down the Frankston line.

By my senior year, I started to enjoy the uncommon feeling of comradeship among my classmates. But academically, I was dog-paddling in footy shorts. Two of my five subjects were too much like chores. Biology was so boring to me I hardly attended classes. I could still handle maths and I liked the teacher, Mr Zahra. But I couldn't understand how the maths we did applied to the real world, so my effort dropped to minimal. I took a hell of a lot of toilet breaks. Sometimes I went twice in the same hour. By doing that, and arriving late, I figured I could cut class time down to about thirty-five minutes.

Even I had to admit my back-up plan of studying law was looking unlikely.

For the three subjects I liked, it helped that I respected my teachers. Mr O'Brien taught Legal Studies. He was a fascinating man, prone to wearing a white skivvy tucked into his jeans. He'd only recently grown out his moustache so he could twirl and wax it at the ends. No one I knew would dare do that, except Mr O'Brien – he was a towering, fearless figure. Even the most cynical teenagers had to admire his commitment to teaching. At first, I thought Mr O'Brien's course might be dull, but he won me over with his assignments, which included a close look at the merits of mandatory reporting of child sexual abuse. I knew this was important because Mum talked to me about it in relation to her work.

English was easy, and made entertaining by Mrs Golden, a no-nonsense teacher who reminded me of all my beloved aunties, Mum's sisters. Mrs Golden had short, wavy hair and warm blue eyes. She knew I enjoyed writing short stories and praised my work, without going overboard. She also knew I could be lazy and arrogant. She was entitled to berate me for that but preferred constructive criticism. She was often on my back to make sure I rewrote my work and took the time to avoid grammatical errors. She placed emphasis on words and how they could be shifted in sentences to add more meaning; to create an authentic storytelling voice. *My* voice. I tried to make Mrs Golden proud, which was more valuable to me than high grades.

In English literature, it was all the more so. Only once did I visibly disappoint Mrs Mac. She had given us a brief writing exercise: to pen our obituaries. I didn't take it seriously and scribbled some rambling sentences without introspection: something about being a millionaire, winning a few Brownlow medals, living to a hundred and being married many times to perennially young wives.

The truth was I didn't want to contemplate my death or hypothetical legacy. It was easier to play the role of a blasé, footy-obsessed boofhead.

Mrs Mac didn't appreciate my obituary. She challenged me on several points. I had no defence, because I thought it was a mindless task. Digging in, I told her, 'I don't care what happens in the future. I just want one hundred thousand people at my funeral. Then I'll know it's been worth it.'

Mrs Mac shot back. 'If you want a lot of people at your funeral,' she said, 'you'd better die young.'

I was taken aback and, for once, fell silent in thought.

15

Sam and Me

After literature one day, Adam and I saw a girl standing against our lockers. She seemed to be waiting for us.

'It's Sam Rowe,' Adam whispered, with reverence. 'I heard she broke up with Kenny.'

I hadn't seen Sam all summer; no one had. She'd become an enigma. But when she was around, she stood out. Athletic, smart and fashionable, Sam was so trendy she changed her hairstyle every year. Today, her smooth, jet-black hair was parted in the middle, falling either side of her face, as if to frame it. She was wearing a white T-shirt under a black jacket. She looked more like a woman than a girl my age. I became self-conscious of my shorts and sneakers – little boy clothes. There were some drinking taps beside Sam, and I took a sip to appear casual.

'Hi,' she said to me. 'Got a sec?'

My pulse jumped a gear. My mouth was instantly dry again.

Adam patted me on the back. 'Catch ya later.'

We made some small talk about Adam and his ex-girlfriend Emma. She was surprised they had split up.

'What about you? You got a girlfriend?' she said.

I shook my head.

'Did you hear Kenny and I broke up?'

'Nup.'

She'd been with Kenny for at least a year, an age in high school. They were a reclusive, talked-about couple. People said they wagged a lot to go down to the beach together. It was one of those suggestive rumours no one questioned.

'Do you know why?' Sam said.

'No.'

'Because of you.'

'What did I do?'

'I like you.'

I wouldn't have been more surprised if she'd told me she burnt down the science wing.

'Oh.'

'Want to go out some time, or come round to my place?'

My mind raced. I nodded as casually as I could manage. 'I've got training most nights, I'll have to let you know.'

She reached out to touch my arm, causing my blood to start charging. 'I look forward to it,' she said.

Sam lived with her mother and sisters, not far from Adam's place. Late one afternoon a few days later, I rode my bike around there. I wore baggy tracksuit pants, an old Reebok T-shirt, and my Greg Chappell cricket hat. In the history of first dates, had anyone ever turned up looking so uncool? Problem was, I had no choice. I didn't want anyone at home to know what I was up to. If I'd dressed up in jeans and polo shirt, Mum would've asked where I was going. I never talked to my parents about girls, and they never asked. I didn't want to ask Steve for any tips because then he'd know how hopeless I was around the opposite sex. So I wore my usual outfit, and hoped Sam wouldn't care.

She was in her driveway, waiting. 'Well, hello,' she said. 'This is a good look. Trackie dacks, really?'

She was wearing fitted blue jeans.

Sam teased me some more and I played along. We were more comfortable in each other's company than we were at school. I noticed she was inching closer to me and I told myself not to move away. We were eye to eye. I had wet palms. I was gabbling; telling her about how often I'd ridden past her place. She didn't ask me in. She said her mum was home. Then she leaned in to kiss me, right there on the driveway pavers. I closed my eyes. Is there anything better than a first kiss? Sam was strong and she controlled our movements. I let her.

Between kissing, we hugged. I didn't want to let go in case she told me this was some sort of prank.

The spell was broken when Sam made another crack about my tracksuit pants. We both looked down at them. Casually, she grabbed my elastic waistband and extended it, as if she were opening a desk drawer.

'Nice,' she said, peering inside.

Taken aback, I replied too formally. 'Thank you. It's okay.' Was I was being measured or compared?

'It's not at full mast, is it?' she said. Finally, she stopped looking down.

'No way,' I said. 'Half-mast at most.'

I knew my mast well. I even measured it once with a wooden school ruler. (Did every boy do that?) Sam seemed to enjoy making me uncomfortable. I didn't take it personally. I was happy to entertain her, still buzzing from our kiss.

Louise was the only other girl I'd ever pashed like this. Before her, I'd briefly been with one of Kate's friends, and kissed a girl at the Frankston circus; neither were fun because my big teeth seemed to get in the way.

I wasn't a complete novice. I read *Cosmopolitan* and *Cleo* magazines (my sisters' copies, and the ones in the doctor's waiting room). I'd gone close to losing my virginity a few times but it was always after drunken parties, on someone's lawn, or in a strange bedroom, fumbling around in the dark. Of course, I carried a condom in my wallet, just in case. All the boys I knew carried 'dingers' (this was our preferred name; Franger was our home, not our contraception). We'd all seen the Grim Reaper AIDS awareness ads on TV, and we all knew the basketball legend Magic Johnson had tested positive to HIV by this stage. Apparently, anyone could get it.

A few years earlier, I'd accidentally signed up for a sex education class when I chose a Year 9 elective called 'personal development'. I could live to be one hundred and fifty and never forget our first lesson. Adam, Leigh and Doc took the class with me. No girls turned up. The school's art teacher, Ms Davies, was in charge. She was one of the best: commanding and passionate. Even so, I imagined she was coerced into this sex-ed experiment. She began by asking us to tell her all the names we knew for vaginas.

'Get it out your system,' she said. 'Then we can get on with learning.' I wondered how long it might take for someone to break the awkward silence. Then two older kids in the back row (they'd stayed down a level) started things off.

'Cunt,' one of them said.

'Pussy,' said the other.

Ms Davies wrote the words on her whiteboard.

'Box,' the first boy said.

'Worm burner,' said his mate.

And they were away, shocking and educating us all. Some of the terms they spouted I'd never heard before, or since. Where did these kids come from, youth detention? To her credit, Ms Davies kept writing. Half the board was filled in no time.

'Okay,' she said. 'What about some words for penis?'

The back row pair were up to the task. Dick. Cock. Rod. Prick. Shlong. Trouser snake. Blue-veined custard pumper. We were falling off our chairs laughing by now. Our all-knowing classmates were enjoying their academic apex.

Ms Davies, mortified by what she was hearing but not one to surrender, kept writing until there was no more space on the board. I reckon those two boys up the back came up with a hundred words and phrases for genitalia, though I can't remember if they ever offered up 'mast'.

In the driveway, Sam had taken my hand in hers.

'Want to go for a walk?' she said.

'Sure.'

We wandered around to our old primary school, a few hundred metres away. We sat on a log fence and watched the sky darken over the rooftops.

'Do people talk about me?' she said.

'What do you mean?' My arm was around her waist.

'Just wondering.'

I said that people liked her. She smiled.

'I remember when we were little, you gave me a hard time,' she said.

'We were in Grade 4,' I said. 'I probably just liked you and didn't know how to show it.'

'Yeah, but you were mean.'

We talked about the morning the other boys and I frightened her on the way into school.

'I'm sorry I was like that,' I said. 'That's shit.'

'It's okay.'

The last glow of sun had faded from view. As the streetlights came to life, Sam and I reminisced. We talked about growing up in Seaford, her parents' divorce. We laughed about getting paired up when we had line dancing. 'You were terrible,' she said. We kissed some more.

Walking slowly back to her house, Sam invited me inside. Her mother was still there but it didn't seem to matter anymore.

After a quick introduction, Sam led me into her bedroom. She sat on her bed and I sat on the floor. She was laughing. 'Did you think we were gunna have sex?' she said.

'Not really.' It was true. I didn't even anticipate the kissing. I guessed she was trying to see if I was disappointed. I wasn't. The evening had turned out better than I imagined. It was relaxed and natural, and I liked Sam more than ever. She didn't seem too grown up anymore. It felt like we were closer to equals.

'I wish we'd talked more over the years,' I told her. It seemed we'd wasted all that time.

'Will you tell your friends you came around?' she said as I headed off.

'Probably just Adam.'

'Do you wanna do this again?'

'That'd be nice,' I said.

I never went back to Sam's house. I was never really sure why. Our friendship was unusual, based on childish crushes, but it felt real enough, so why didn't I honour it? Was I put off by her having more romantic experience? Was it like what Thomas Hardy said about Tess? Maybe I was no better than those establishment arseholes in that old book. No, that wasn't it. It was more that I wanted to fall deeply in love with a girl — like characters did in movies. I wanted that girl to be someone I met unexpectedly, someone who didn't know what I used to be like. And I wanted to have sex for the first time with that girl. I'd been waiting so long — for love and sex — I'd started to romanticise both. My biggest problem was that I didn't know what love felt like. I wrote about it my diary, right next to another passage of longing about Louise. 'Will there be anyone at all that I can love?' But love had to be more than what I felt for Louise. It had to be. Because my feelings for her were fading too.

I knew it was a shame and I knew it was my fault that I didn't pursue lasting friendships with girls whose company I enjoyed, like Samantha Rowe. We had a lot in common, and Sam was more fun to be with than a lot of blokes I hung around with. Steve had female friends; both my sisters seemed to have male friends. They made it look easy. But I withdrew from Sam at every opportunity. We barely spoke to each other for the rest of the year. It was part of my instinctive reaction to girls trying to connect to me. I was either all-in or all-out. It denied me the chance to get to know any of them on an emotional level. I didn't like it, but I didn't know how to change.

I lost my virginity about a month later at a party a few suburbs away. I woke up the next day not remembering the girl's name;

I doubt she remembered mine. In a rush to lose my innocence before I turned eighteen, I had wimped out and taken the easiest path, and I regretted it immediately.

16

The Club

Boys are delivered twice. Once into our mothers' arms, then into the care of male elders; role models we seek beyond our fathers. For me it was Steve and his friends, the hard-drinking blokes of the local football club, a beacon of Australian male culture.

Though I was playing for the Stingrays, I was going back to my Seaford footy club on Saturday nights with my own mates. Every weekend felt like a homecoming, and I liked the way the local guys asked me about my prospects at the higher level. Not that they treated me as special – the opposite was true – but they seemed to recognise that I was talented and commited. At every social function, they welcomed me into the social rooms with pats on the back and a can of (Jim) Beam. I loved being one of the Seaford boys. Outside playing footy, it was my most comfortable place. The club was always jumping. Some of their weekend parties were the best I've ever seen. As an athlete, I told myself that nights like these were just a bit of harmless fun – all part of the post-game wind-down. After a few sips of those sweet black drinks ('mother's milk', we called it), I didn't even bother with justifications. I knew that carrying on like this was unhealthy. I knew it was irreconcilable with my aim of making the grade in AFL. But the temptation was too great. I was happy here. I was doing what I wanted.

The Stingrays had played two games since our opening round loss to Central Dragons. Both had been defeats. The second game was against Ballarat Rebels at home. My performance had been adequate. Hutchy said I didn't look as 'switched on'. The following week, however, we took on the Northern Knights, and I played the game of my life.

It was at Princes Park – home ground of AFL teams Carlton and Fitzroy. The Knights had a band of the best young footballers in the country. One of them was Matthew Blagrove, who'd impressed league recruiters while playing for Victoria in the previous Under 17 National Championships; another was John Barker, so good he'd already been picked up to play for Fitzroy (he was allowed to play in the Under 18s when Fitzroy didn't select him). Within minutes of the first bounce it was obvious to anyone watching that Northern was a superior side to ours. The golden-haired Blagrove was everything they said he'd be. He moved easily, grimacing (or was he smiling?) as he ran with the ball. Barker was a colossus in the forward line. And, as it turned out, the Knights had other brilliant teenagers: strapping centre-half-forward Jarrod Molloy (who would make his name with Fitzroy, Brisbane and Collingwood), and sleek ruck rover Angelo Lekkas (a future Hawthorn stalwart).

The ball spent almost the entire game in our backline, which meant I was always within a kick of the action. When Hutchy realised we were going to struggle to surge up the field, he sent our key forward Smithy to strengthen our defence. It was the Stingrays' version of the Batman signal. For the rest of the match, I was The Caped Crusader's sidekick, without the green duds. The presence of Smithy gave me confidence to play on any opponent. We kept switching matchups. At one point I was sent to Barker. 'You take the big fella,' Crouchy said. Really? With no hope of outmarking him from behind, I stayed in front but close enough to touch his jumper; this position gave me an advantage when the ball came at us along the ground. I swooped on a few crumbs, ran and kicked long into space. I had some good fortune along the way. The ball seemed to bounce my way more often than usual. In sport, you can have one of those days when the ball seems to belong to you – everything slows down – and you can see its trajectory ahead of time. It's a consequence of being relaxed but focused, a rare state of mind that comes to you, rather than the other way around. My senses were so alive against the Knights I was able to stand at the member's end and position myself in front of my opponent, anticipating his moves before he made them, watching his shadow on the grass. I cut off nearly every attack they sent my way.

Smithy was a marvel that day. He must have taken at least twenty marks. I could see he was enjoying himself. His self-belief gave him free rein in the second half and, as the game opened up, he didn't bother manning up in defence. It wasn't in his nature to play on someone. They could play on him. And when the ball came near, he won it. His grip was unbreakable.

We still lost by seven goals, but I felt honoured to have shared the afternoon with so many players who were better than me. Some of them went on to play in the AFL seniors, although Blagrove wasn't one of them. He came close, bobbing up in the reserves for Essendon and Carlton. Not that I needed to see him starring on TV; in my mind I can still replay visions of him from that game – swerving at full speed, captivating us all, hair flipping and flopping, teeth gritted, to finish with five goals.

After the game I'd heard Crouchy tell someone, 'We would've lost by twenty goals if it wasn't for Smithy and PK.' I couldn't have been prouder to hear my name mentioned alongside Shayne Smith than if I'd just been named captain of Collingwood. When the *Herald Sun* ran its next big spread on our league, I searched for the coaches' votes. It read: '5. M Blagrove (N), 4. A Lekkas (N), 3. S Smith (S), 2. J Molloy (N), 1. P Kennedy (S).'

I owed a lot to my Seaford footy club roots. I had first watched a senior game when I was about ten. The local derbies against nearby Pines attracted a thousand people or more. The footballers seemed like fearless giants. At local level, this was still the era of king hits and all-in brawls. A player could barely exist in this arena without being able to fight, or at least bluster. But the biggest jolt for any youngster coming into the senior club to play Under 17s (as I did when I was still only fifteen) was the off-field indoctrination.

Communal showering after training sessions and games was the first daunting challenge. Everyone sized up each other's dicks. The bigger boys showed off with penis wristwatches and did soap-lathered helicopters. Some fellas got their nicknames courtesy of their generous appendages. 'Mr Ed'. 'Slonk'. Smaller boys were ridiculed and expected to laugh along. The hazards didn't end there when you were in the David Gower (shower). You had to be aware of who was beside you because some teenagers liked to piss on each other, using the warm water as cover. I got peed on. It made me furious. The club tolerated the knob-based taunts, but it drew the line at literal piss-taking; when the senior coach caught a serial pisser, he threatened to beat the shit out him. That slowed the flow for a while.

These were hijinks common to most clubs, as far as I knew. Then there were the conventions we learnt in the social rooms at Seaford footy club, where beer, bourbon, ouzo and scotch were the beverages of choice, and people drank to oblivion. Our suburb was well known as the booze capital of the Frankston area. The Seaford Hotel (previously The Sundowner, aka 'The Gundowner' – because someone apparently got shot there) regularly topped the state for liquor sales.

Adam often joined me for the big Saturday nights at the Seaford footy club. So did two other mates, Juan Merchan and Leo Bellodi. They both went to Frankston's biggest Catholic school, John Paul College (with my teammate Jeff White, among other mutual friends). Juan was Spanish–Australian, and a natural ladies' man. He once told me his secret to wooing girls: 'I just talk to them. Whisper in their ears. They love it.' It helped that he was athletic and good looking. Leo was the son of an Italian taxi driver and a doting mother. He was as intelligent as anyone I knew, and sarcastic. I laughed at his social commentary on the world as loud as I laughed at Adam's. Our favourite shared pastime was to sit at the bar and eat cashews, while Leo predicted and then witnessed other boys' failed pick-up attempts. Of course, we knew the joke was on us: at least those blokes were having a go.

Adam, Juan and Leo had all played alongside me in the Seaford Under 17s. We were already junior members of the larger tribe. This was our path into manhood. We took it because we wanted, more anything else, to be men.

Our Saturday nights started at dusk, and we often went

without dinner. There was a saying: 'Eatin's cheatin'.' It meant you get drunk quicker on an empty stomach.

Adam, Juan, Leo and I liked to get tipsy before arriving at any function. We mixed bottles of spirits with soft drink in plastic bottles. We sang songs on the way to the club. Listening to Adam sing while getting a buzz from cheap liquor was even better than doing it sober. Between songs, we told each other what a great night we were going to have.

Comedy nights were popular at the club; the braver emerging stand-up acts fronting up to pressure-test their material on five hundred boozed-up locals in a small, smoke-filled room. Everyone from that time remembers a young comic making our cheeks hurt for days with his jokes about being on the dole. No one had heard of him, but Dave Hughes would later become a national sensation on stage and radio.

But most celebrated of all was the Annual Players' Revue, where the senior footballers performed random acts, often wearing dresses and lip-syncing pop songs. I remember one performance above all the others; it said everything about the time and the place.

When we got to the club on the night of this particular revue, we could hear the music from the street. The fact that I had a Stingrays game the next day – our first Sunday match of the year – was drowned out by the nightclub atmosphere.

'It's pumpin',' Juan said.

We paid our ten bucks to get in; the doorman stamped our hands. The social rooms were cramped, so full you couldn't move without squeezing sideways through the crowd. Leo was bopping his head to the music, surveying the throng with approval. 'Fuck yeah, heaps of chicks.' As fashion dictated, the blokes were in jeans, with patterned shirts or plain polos; the young women were similarly attired – jeans, floral shirts or turtleneck tops. There was a lot of crimped hair, which I reckoned looked hot.

Carving a path to the bar, I ordered four Beam cans. I saw Steve in the crowd. Jo was there too, with her boyfriend Ash. I had a drink or two with my older siblings. It was good to talk to them, even though we had to shout to be heard. Kate was the only one missing; she was a year away from joining us for these types of nights.

The bourbon went straight to my head. I gave into it. My whole body loosened, and my brain's light faded. I let it dim. In this state of mind, I could forget about any cares that had built up over the week and I could mix easily with the groggy crowd. Most of the talk among the boys and men was about girls and women. Men perved with singular focus and rated the females in the room on their looks and movements. It was a grown-up version of the games we played in the schoolyard, only the language was harsher. I mimicked the words and sentences I picked up from others. Young females were chicks, birds, moles, or sluts, depending on how they were categorised by those who seemed to know. We used these words casually and pretended they were okay. We knew it was just as offensive here as it was back in school. Men didn't talk like that in front of loved ones – girlfriends, sisters, mothers or wives. No one ever dared call Jo a mole, or worse, in front of my brother and me. Steve and I would have stood toe to toe with anyone who dared. We had our family honour to protect.

Our language also framed our constant discussions about sexual conquest, real or imagined. Celebrated were the players who boasted about having outdoor sex in the coaches' box, a tiny tin shed beside the oval. Some of the single players had their own unofficial competition, called 'Pog Lotto', whose winner was determined by the man who had sex with a woman declared to be the least attractive. I never heard anyone denounce the contest, nor did I think it was a real thing; it was one of those endless jokes some males used to put females down, and make insecure young blokes feel better about their failures. I kept quiet about my true romantic sensitivities. I was always getting asked the question: 'Ya on the prowl?'

'Bloody oath,' was my answer.

I wouldn't have dared reply open-heartedly: 'Actually, mate, I'm hoping to get hit by Cupid's arrow any day now.'

Curiously, the conquest complex didn't permeate my group of close friends. Adam, Juan, Leo and I were more likely to talk self-deprecatingly about our lack of success. It was a running joke that eased tension around the topic. Juan was an exception. Girls seemed comfortable talking to him and he had an ease that I envied. I wondered whether it had something to do with his European bloodlines. In some parts of the world, men are taught to love women.

The players' revue acts started late. The crowd was drunk and happy. I remember the showstopping final performance like it was last night. I was at the back of the audience, standing on a table to see over the heads of those at the front.

The actors were a couple of clever and popular players called Spud and Fletch. They meandered onto a makeshift wooden stage carrying pieces of paper, which turned out to be lyrics to a song they had written. Or rather, rewritten. Music started playing. I recognised it as the tune to 'That's Amore'.

A few whistles went up, then some shooshes. Spud held the microphone. He and Fletch began singing the words. Instead of 'That's Amore', they went with 'That's a Whore-ay'.

People around me winced. A few sniggered.

'You can tell by her smell that she's not very well, that's a whore-ay.'

'That's harsh,' someone said. More people laughed. I laughed. After a couple more lines, there were more smiles than blank looks. Spud and Fletch were buoyed. They kept going – the song went on and on. We started singing along. 'That's a whore-ay!' There was generous applause. I can't remember how many women were still there while this was going on. There must have been dozens. It never occurred to me to look at their reactions. When it was finished, Spud and Fletch received a standing ovation.

After the show, the music got even louder, and I tried to dance. I'd started cadging ciggies and was blowing smoke as I lurched to the beats. The bourbon had done its job. I'd handed over the controls to my senses hours earlier. I felt free, unleashed. When Dexy's Midnight Runners hit the speakers with 'Come on Eileen', I jumped up and down. We sang so loud we might've loosened the plaster on the ceiling. I felt all grown up and wild, without fear, insecurity or doubt.

That night, I spoke to a girl named Cassie. We remembered each other from primary school. I told her she used to have pigtails. 'Weird seeing you after so long,' I said. 'How's things?' I would never have remembered this conversation if it didn't lead to a tumultuous event months later.

It was past midnight when the crowd started thinning. Almost everyone was going to kick on at the Frankston pubs. I was sitting, exhausted, at a table, nursing a half-empty glass. I wasn't at blackout stage but I wasn't far off it. A headache was coming on. I contemplated vomiting in the toilet, cleaning out my stomach. One of Steve's friends dropped into a chair in front of me. His name was Anthony, but we all knew him as Ant. He'd grown up in the estate next to mine. He also happened to be the younger brother of my St Kilda footy hero, Robert Harvey.

'What are you still doing here?' Ant said. 'You've got footy tomorrow.'

The Stingrays were due to play Murray Bushrangers, in Seymour – which meant a two-hour, early-morning bus trip north, to the town where I was born. Ant knew I should have been in bed hours ago. 'What time is it?' I looked at my watch and gave him a bleary smile. 'No hurry.'

'It's not funny,' Ant said. He seemed angry for some reason.

'What's the problem? You're still here too,' I said.

'My game was *today*,' he said. Like his brother, Ant played for St Kilda. He'd just been drafted into the AFL reserves. 'You've got a game tomorrow. What are you trying to prove?'

'Fuck it,' I said. 'I don't really care.' My addled brain didn't appreciate Ant's line of questioning. Why wasn't he cutting me some slack? He'd been at the local footy club and pubs with the rest of us. What was his problem?

'You *do* care,' he said. 'I know you do. Go home. Stop drinking and stop fucking smoking. Take your footy seriously.'

His words cut through my drunken fug. He saw past my bullshit bravado. I tried to hide the humiliation I felt in his rebuke.

I walked home alone, unsteady and shamefaced.

17

Dad's Footsteps

———————

Early the next morning, Dad drove me to the bus stop. He didn't mention my big night out, rather he began reminiscing about Seymour. He talked about our family's early years living at the nearby army base at Puckapunyal, where he'd worked after leaving the navy.

Dad always laughed when he remembered life at 'Pucka'. He had three jobs, including his army duties. On weekends, he was a cab driver, ferrying pissed soldiers from the Seymour pubs back to the army base. One of the drunks made a big impression on him by vomiting in his back seat. On weeknights, he drove the local abattoir truck to the city to dump all the hooves, heads, guts and blood. This was a four-hour round trip for which he was paid fifteen bucks. The offal was usually sitting in the sun for an hour or so before he picked it up. Only the flies were pleased with this. He had to climb into the cabin of the 'stink truck' so the blowies didn't come in with him. Dad once tried to do the right thing and stop at the highway truck weighbridge near the Seymour on-ramp but was frantically waved away by a man holding his nose and yelling: 'Keep fucking going!'

My parents had only one regret from their time in Seymour.

Not that they had any control over it. In 1974, a year before I was born, Mum had a miscarriage. She confided years later that the baby would have been a boy. For a while after she told me I imagined that the baby was real and he had died, and that our family was one short. I knew I was being selfish. When you're a kid you can never have too many friends to play with. After Kate was born, Dad got the snip. There was some talk later about him having a reversal, but he ended up saying it wasn't on.

Dad left the army after six years, as I was starting to run around after my brown plastic football. His exit was unexpectedly painful. He hurt his back and was laid up in a repatriation hospital for months. Sometimes all he could do to manage the pain was lie down in the lounge and elevate his legs on the wall. It scared me to see such a strong man, my Superman, crippled. I held my breath for him. These bouts of incapacitation came and went. Each time, Dad willed himself back to health. And I could exhale.

18

Getting Away with it

In Seymour, where the gum trees seemed as big as city buildings, we played somewhere near our best from the first bounce. We were desperate to record our first win, and it showed. Following Hutchy's instructions to play on and handball as much as possible, we were surging forward in pairs and trios. Our opponents, the Bushrangers, seemed stunned. We were looking and feeling more threatening.

Thanks to a sleep on the bus, the worst of my hangover had cleared. My base fitness was still holding up. Once again, the ball seemed to bounce my way. Running alongside me was one of our rising stars, the quirky Dean Watson (Watto). Though introverted off the field, he was assertive during games. He was also fast and arguably our best endurance athlete. No one could keep up with him; he won more of the ball as matches wore on, and other boys got tired. He was a free-ranging player, long striding and unpredictable. Spectators called him the 'sideways man' because he was always searching for space on the wings. In this regard, he was ahead of his time. But he also had a knack of kicking goals. Brett Anthony (BA) was Watto's midfield running mate, but the similarities ended there. BA was a muscular, short-legged player, who was always in motion. Self-assured and respected, he'd left school and was working as a trades apprentice. His streetfighter look belied his soft, skilful touch. I always ran past him when he had the Sherrin; he shot out handballs as neatly wrapped gifts.

If BA and Watto could dominate the midfield, we could make the most of our biggest weapon: Smithy. He was getting better every game. An eye-popping haul of marks for any game was about ten; Smithy averaged fifteen. After training one night, he had challenged me to a marking duel. 'See how many you can take out of twenty,' he said. Crouchy kicked the ball to us from about thirty metres away. I didn't take one mark. Smithy took nineteen. I was able to spoil him once. It was a brutal demolition, but I couldn't be mad. His prowess was awe-inspiring, almost beautiful: each time the ball landed in his hands it sounded like someone sitting down on a leather sofa. It was also the closest I ever came to making a real connection with my most admired teammate. I wished he could defeat me like that every week. But he never asked me again.

At Seymour oval we kicked nine goals in the first quarter, three in the second, ten in the third and six in the fourth – to win by eighty-two points. Smithy took mark after mark, kicking three goals and sharing the spoils among teammates. Watto had a day out too, collecting thirty-one possessions. But our best player was a teenager I'd never seen before, John Barnett. (A listed Hawthorn player who wasn't required by the Hawks reserves that weekend, he would go on to play for North Melbourne and Collingwood.) His movement and self-confidence were a class above. In shades of Dad and his stink truck, Barnett yelled at me at one point to follow up one of my kicks. 'Don't just stand there, keep going.'

The only bad decision I made against the Bushrangers was in the last quarter. Careering into an opponent's knee, I corked my thigh so badly I could hardly stand up by the final siren. Blood congealed in my numb leg.

The win would move us from tenth on the ladder to seventh. For the first time, our coach was smiling after the game. 'I expect you boys to show that type of commitment every week. We won three quarters today… but we've gotta start producing four solid quarters if we wanna keep winning.'

At the post-match function, I limped up to receive an award as one of the best players. It was an honour, but in some ways, it was the last thing I needed. I needed a young man like Ant Harvey in my ear, letting me know that I'd got away with it, this time. The boy who succeeds by acting recklessly thinks it's his right to do it again and again without consequences.

But for now, I was immortal, and the bus ride home was pure joy. I was feeling a big part of a special team. Awkward pre-season silences had been replaced by laughter. This felt like the beginning of something exciting.

There was another reason we were buzzing. Hutchy had explained to us that the representative season was coming. Some of the bottom-age boys had been selected in the Victorian Under 17 Teal Cup Squad; they would be competing in a national championship. Five more of us had been asked to train with an Under 18 Victorian metropolitan team for a one-off match at the MCG in early June. We were slated to play a curtain raiser before the AFL State of Origin grand final.

It was really happening.

19

Clueless

———————

I noticed more cop cars going this way and that along Frankston–
Cranbourne Road. It was normal to see them now.

The police presence in our suburbs had grown with the
frustrations of finding no clues left by the killer of Elizabeth
Stevens. It seemed to anyone following the news updates that the
Lloyd Park killer was in the wind, maybe gone forever.

But the Elizabeth Stevens mannequin was still there on the
side of the road. It was like an all-too-real scene from *Twin Peaks*.
Detectives, who still didn't even know for sure that Elizabeth had
been on the bus, reached out to the local youth for answers. They
wanted to hear from teenagers who had been playing video games
at popular hangouts like Frankston's Timezone, and the pool hall
across the road. Have you seen this girl? Think hard. These were
places I knew well. But apparently no one had seen Elizabeth in
the hours before she died. Not one person. Somewhere, I suspected,
the murderer was laughing at the cops.

The *Frankston Standard*'s 'Street Poll' section quoted worried
residents who lived close to the murder scene. One lady said she
was reluctant to go outside in the dark. A thirty-four-year-old
mother said she now looked at other people differently. Another

woman said it was 'too close to home', and that until now she thought Langwarrin was 'a nice suburb'.

I thought all the suburbs surrounding Frankston were nice, including ours.

Round our way growing up, divorce was just about the scariest thing I'd heard about. Jo wrote about it in an anniversary card to our parents when she was eight. 'To Mum and Dad, I love you and 10 years is a long time to be married and with not 1 split up, but if there were I don't know who to go with because I love you both very much.'

'You can't write that,' I told my older sister. I thought she might be tempting fate.

'Watch me,' she said.

Now, divorce was as common as marriage. But murder was new to me. While I was struggling to believe it was possible that a girl my age could be slain while walking down the street, I was beginning to grasp the inequity. No one was waiting for me in the dark.

20

Jobless

Whether he meant to or not, my manager at Kentucky got his revenge on me soon after Adam and I had dined out on free fried chicken. Craig had rung our house one night, desperate for me to do a fill-in shift right away.

I told him I was about to sit down to a State of Origin rugby league match with my father. Dad, always a Sydney boy at heart, had instilled in me a love for both rugby codes. I was one of the few Victorian supporters of Canterbury-Bankstown and New South Wales. I also loved watching the Wallabies, whose 1991 World Cup win hooked me for life.

'That's not an excuse,' Craig said. He seemed more authoritative than usual. 'Get in here now.'

'It's a very good excuse,' I said. 'I've been looking forward to this game for weeks.'

I spared Craig the details, but my sporting devotions ranged far and wide. On top of the rugby, I was positively giddy about the upcoming Ashes test series in England. It was only weeks away. Dean Jones had been dropped from the Australian team but another Victorian, Shane Warne, was in. I wasn't sure if the leg spinner was going to be any good over there, but I was going to stay up all night during the tests to watch him anyway. (On the second day of this test series, Warne would announce his sporting genius by bowling his 'Ball of the Century' to Mike Gatting.)

'When does the match start?' Craig asked. 'Can't you tape it and watch it later?'

The game was hours away. I could have worked a shift and been home in time for kick off, but Craig's tone got my back up.

'I'm not coming in,' I said.

'Well, if you want work here anymore you will,' he said.

'You can't sack me. You didn't give me enough notice. I know my rights.'

'No, I can't sack you. But I do the rosters and I don't have to put you down on them. So, are you working tonight or not?'

'Nah,' I said. My pride wouldn't allow it. 'Thanks anyway.'

Suddenly I was unemployed. Without an income, I had to rearrange my finances. My expenses were drinking and renting videos; giving up my big Saturday nights was not an option, so I decided to limit my movie rentals and make a special effort to return the ones I did rent on time to avoid late fees. I also had to find other things to do on lonely weekday nights when I didn't have training. Something free.

21

Owl Calls

Not long after the Seymour game – still nursing a corked thigh – I went to bed early and started writing a short story in my diary. When I got stumped for words, I put down my pen and did something unusual. I picked up a novel. *I Heard the Owl Call My Name*. It was the book Mrs Mac had given me.

I read the cover quote ('an epic quality... an entrancing chemistry' – *NEW YORK TIMES*) then checked how many pages it was from cover to cover. It was one hundred and thirty-three. Not a lot. Bugger it. I'll give it a go. Part One was called *Yes, my lord – no, my lord*. Jesus, I thought, not a churchie book. I had no time for religion. I wasn't an atheist, as such. It was just that faith wasn't a big deal in our home. Mum once sent Steve and me to Sunday school at a small weatherboard Uniting Church near Seaford railway station. We must have been about six and eight. When Mum came to wake us the following Sunday morning, we didn't budge. We had already planned to fake sleep at all costs. 'Up you get,' Mum said. 'Stop pretending.' But to our surprise, she left it at that. She never mentioned church again. That was it for Him and me, which suited me just fine, because Sundays were for footy anyway.

To my eternal surprise, the book's cover quote was no exaggeration. From the first page, the words were magical. Reading them was like rubbing Aladdin's lamp.

He stood at the wheel, watching the current stream, and the bald eagles fishing for herring that waited until the boat was almost upon them to lift, to drop the instant it had passed. The tops of the islands were wreathed in cloud, the sides fell steeply, and the firs that covered them grew so precisely to the high tide line that now, at slack, the up-coast of British Columbia showed its bones in a straight selvage of wet, dark rock.

I was swept away to a wild place, far beyond anything I was familiar with. I couldn't tell whether it was America or Canada. It didn't matter. The author Margaret Craven, my handholding guide, encouraged me to look up at the mountains and down into the water and across at the sharp rocks. She wanted me to meet her characters, who were gentle and honest and true. The novel held me in a trance. I was in it, riding on a boat with a pale young priest, Mark Brian, who was sent to a remote village by a wise bishop. The young priest is terminally ill. The bishop knows this, but the young man doesn't. Through Craven's magnetic descriptions, I was able to become a friend of the village's dying traditions, and the dying young man. I learnt to sit and watch.

For many pages I was as sad and lonely as Mark himself. I surprised myself by crying several times; sometimes I was happy, sometimes mournful. When Mark spent the 'last lovely days of September' looking for salmon in the streams above the village, I sat shivering on the river's rocks, peering into the clear waters, willing the fish into view.

As I turned each page, I became aware of them running out.

I tried to read slower to prolong my time in the village. It was getting late in my house, but I didn't look at the clock.

He waited patiently as if he had waited all his life, as if he were part of time itself.

I stayed with Mark until the owl called his name, and we both knew it was his time to die.

This story made its way into my marrow. Previously, I was too restless to settle into novels without being pushed. I liked some of our assigned books – *Cloudstreet* by Tim Winton comes to mind – although I felt I wasn't clever enough to find the magic in them. Craven's book seemed on a different scale. Her words transcended the page; her story seemed so rich in colour that I could touch and smell the world she imagined for me. I could hear her whispering to me. I could sense the animals in the forest. Only once did I curse the writer: when she let Mark die. By then I felt like I was fading too.

I didn't want to leave the village. I'd become determined to stay and live my life in the service of others. I was going to be gentler, kinder.

At the end, when I stopped crying, I decided I wanted to be a Margaret Craven; to tell wise stories. But I could never match Craven. That would be like trying to run as fast as Carl Lewis. I could, however, find my own way as a writer. I was already practising in my scrapbook journal. Thinking about the possibilities of it gave me a floating sensation that I'd only ever had while daydreaming of football. Until then, nothing in my life came close to that freedom of movement, that elation of physical competition. But I had suspected there might be more to me, or at least to life, waiting for me. Here it was.

I made a pledge to read as many books as I could. Would I have the discipline? Yes, I would have to. In no mood to sleep, I began to read the book again. When my eyelids weighed too heavily, I skipped around, looking for the paragraphs I knew had changed my world.

They moved again and saw the end of the swimmer. They watched her valiant fight for life, her struggle to right herself when the gentle stream turned her, and they watched the water force open her gills and draw her gently downstream, tail first, as she had started to the sea as a fingerling.

I felt electricity in that magnificent, awful scene. I was going to die one day. And I would struggle and fail. And someone would be watching me, unable to help. Where would it end for me? Was it all worth it? It had to be.

… the devil's club put out small new leaves for the deer to nibble, and the bears emerged from their dens, thin, blinking in the light.

When I finally put the book back on the shelf it was three o'clock in the morning. I drifted off into a nightmare, the first I could remember ever having. The scene was a beach under a black and purple sky. I was trying to go for a swim, but the waves were pushing me back onto land. I tried to fight back against the sea, kicking and thrashing in vain. On waking, I scribbled down the details in my diary: 'Beaten for the last time, I sat. And began to think. What if I never get in? What if I'm shut out all my life? I could do nothing else but cry.'

22

The Cut

———

'Close the door behind you, mate.'

I did so without a word in reply. We were in a medical room attached to the footy change room. Windowless, with plain white walls, it was like a prison cell without the bars.

Merv Keane sat across from me, broad jawed and unsmiling. A former Richmond premiership player, he was coach of the Victorian metropolitan Under 18 team. I'd been training with his squad for the past fortnight. Behind him stood another man – it must have been the selector, and former Melbourne, Essendon and Collingwood player, Tony Elshaug – but I didn't look at him.

I didn't know why they had taken me aside like this. The smell of liniment rent the air. I could still hear my teammates goofing around on the other side of the wall. In two days, we'd be playing for Victoria – the Big V – against a country team at the MCG, before the AFL State of Origin grand final between Victoria and South Australia. We were like little kids waiting at the front gates of Disneyland, waving our tickets in the air.

I picked at the white tape wrapped around the hand I broke six months earlier. The bone had long been healed, but the tape had become my superstition. I'd barely played a poor game since I started with it. Why change anything?

After our breakthrough victory in Seymour, the Stingrays had thrashed Gippsland Power in Leongatha. BA and Watto had cut loose in the midfield as if they'd been allocated exclusive rights to the open spaces. Smithy had put on a masterclass up forward, kicking seven goals. With the backline quieter than usual, I'd spent the afternoon sneaking up the ground. I snagged a goal in the second half. The newspaper headline read: 'Stingrays make it two in a row'. Another win followed against the Pioneers in the goldfield town of Bendigo. Newspaper headline: 'Southern gold rush'. During that seventy-five-point victory, Hutchy unearthed another star onballer – wingman Shane Quinn, who upstaged BA and Watto with thirty possessions. Whitey's ruck partner Paul Clements was also starting to show his potential. 'Clemmo' was V-shaped and athletic, with bright red hair and a warm, all-day grin. There was something about our ruckmen; they were always having a good time. They radiated happiness before and after games. I loved being near them.

With our captain Benny as our touchstone, the press was starting to mention our backline as a team within a team. 'Southern's defence held firm with captain Ben Delarue leading the way, with great support from Paul Kennedy, Mick Prentice, Simon Morwood and Adam White.' Prentice was already a highly fancied full-back. Morwood and Adam White (no relation to Jeff) were also fetching accolades.

A week later we lost to the competition-leading Western Jets. Headline: 'Stingrays crash'. Smithy wasn't playing; he'd been called up to fill in for the Sydney Swans reserves team. Another boy – Chad Liddell – kicked four goals and announced himself as a rising star (he would later play for Collingwood as a hard-tackling forward then back-flanker). We were back on the winners' list the next weekend, beating the Ranges by forty-four points in the lead-up to a St Kilda versus West Coast game. My clearest memory of that game was Jeff White soaring onto the shoulders of his opponent before floating back to earth as if he were wearing a parachute, smiling all the way down. Report: 'Southern regulars Shane Quinn, Paul Kennedy and Adam White were again prominent in what turned out to be a most impressive second half display.'

We were almost halfway through the season. And here I was about to play for a Victorian team, alongside some of the best teenage footballers I'd ever seen. But Merv Keane looked too stern for my liking. I suddenly felt claustrophobic.

'Mate, this isn't easy for me,' he said. 'You know what I'm gunna say?'

'Maybe,' I said. I felt sick to my stomach.

'How's ya knee?' Merv said. 'Seems like you might not be a hundred per cent.'

I'd copped a knock the week before at Waverley. I was limping at the end of the game. But the pain had gone.

'Nah, my knee's all right,' I said. 'No worries.'

'Righto,' Merv said. 'But—'

'I'm right to play,' I insisted. I felt the walls pressing in.

Merv sighed heavily. 'I understand this isn't what you want to hear, but we don't want to take any risks going into this game and we reckon your knee's a concern.'

'Fuckin' hell,' I said. My blood charged and I felt the heat in my face. I made fists of my hands, but then caught myself and breathed deeply, let my fingers spread out. 'Sorry.'

I understood that Merv had twenty-five players in the squad, and he could only field twenty-two. Three players had to miss out. But why did it have to be me? I'd trained well. It didn't seem fair to suggest I was injured when I wasn't, although he might have thought I was lying.

'I know you're disappointed,' Merv said. 'But you're still in the squad as an emergency.'

Emergency. It meant I could bring my boots and uniform to the game and play if one of the other boys got injured during the warm-up. That was never going to happen. To me, being an emergency was no better than being just another anonymous spectator. I didn't want to watch from the sidelines. I wanted – I needed! – to play. How would recruiters know what I could do if I wasn't on the MCG with the best players in our league? I blamed Merv. If he knew me, he wouldn't make me an emergency. Then I blamed myself for showing pain when I hurt my knee the week before. Weakness had cost me.

'Yeah, okay,' I said. I could feel tears coming. I stared at the wall, willing the heartache away. I wondered how I would tell my parents that I hadn't made the team.

There was nothing more to say. Merv looked relieved that our conversation was over. I wanted to protest further, but it would have come off as pitiful.

I went next door to join my teammates for a photo shoot, trying to look composed. We wore our Victorian jumpers. I was number twenty-one. As annoyed and disappointed as I was, I was pleased for my Stingrays mates who were in the side. The photographer told us to look happy and I tried in vain. I was never good at faking smiles. After a few seconds I gave up and stared through the lens without any expression. It was a mask for my conflicted emotions: my pride in wearing the Big V, and my embarrassment that it was only for this one moment, cruelly recorded for posterity.

A dinner followed. Guest speaker was Terry Wheeler, coach of Footscray in the AFL. He told us what it took to be a professional football player: perfect practice, fitness (agility, endurance, flexibility), experience (learn from every game), and attitude (adopt a positive approach). He said it was up to young people like us to make our mark on the world. It was an inspiring talk, but it couldn't erase my shame at being left out. By the time I got home that night, I was furious again. The words I wrote in my diary were full of frustration, even hate. I swore revenge on the boys I deemed unworthy, who'd been chosen ahead of me. I made a promise to become fitter and stronger and better. I made plans to go running around the streets again: hill sprints over the railway overpass. I had to be disciplined. No more late nights in Frankston or at the Seaford footy club. No more binge drinking and smoking. I wanted to prove the Merv Keanes of the world wrong.

'By the end of the year everybody will be reading about me,' I wrote, 'not the other bloke.'

Two days later I watched my teammates live out their dreams as they ran out onto the MCG. I bought a *Football Record* for two bucks and sat next to Mum. We turned to the page of team lists. There was my name: 21. Paul Kennedy (Southern Stingrays). I apologised to Mum for not being out there. It was her forty-sixth birthday and I knew that seeing her boy play at the MCG would have been a pretty special present. I had my gear with me; it made me feel like an imposter, so I tucked it under my seat, out of sight. Mum told me not to worry about it and that she loved me.

The metropolitan team beat the country side by a few goals. I didn't care. After the Under 18s match, we stayed to watch the senior game. Seaford's own Robert Harvey was playing for the Vics, as were Gary Ablett, Paul Roos and Jim Stynes. Stephen Kernahan, Craig Bradley and Johnny Platten were all representing the Croweaters. Our boy Harvey was awarded the EJ Whitten Medal for being Victoria's best player.

On the way home, I gazed again at my name in the *Football Record*. I felt fraudulent. I was a non-starter. My dream of playing on the MCG had never seemed so far away.

When I got home, I told my parents I was heading out for the night.

'Make sure you look after yourself,' Mum said. She gave me a worried look. 'Where are you going?'

'The pub,' I said. 'I'll be right.'

'Don't get too drunk,' said Mum. She saw right through me.

I'd already planned it out. Tonight, I was going to banish the past and the future. I was going to drink myself into a timeless state of now; of music, girls, perfume, smoke, violence, hope, fantasy and loneliness. Of nothing.

Hours later, I was paralytic, teetering in my boxer shorts on a table beside a backyard pool with my arms in the air, reciting 'The Last Barman Poet' from *Cocktail*, with a local twist.

'I am the last barman poet. I see Frankston drinking the fabulous cocktails I make. Frankston getting stinky on something I stir or shake ...'

Someone shouted at me, 'Geddown, idiot.'

I was at a house party in the Frankston hills, south of the pubs, overlooking the bay. I couldn't remember arriving at the party. Adam and I must have caught a cab there after drinking at The Grand. Or maybe we walked. I'd been downing mixed spirits at breakneck speed.

'Jump,' someone else yelled.

The cold blue lights of the unheated pool shone up at me as I went on with my recitation.

'… The iced tea, the kamikaze, the orgasm, the death spasm, the Singapore sling, the dingaling.'

Adam was poolside, half-smiling, shaking his head at me and my poem.

'… The sex on the beach, the schnapps made from peach …'

I had no idea whose party it was. The house was fancy; among those I'd seen a thousand times from the highway. More voices were calling for me to jump.

From my vantage point, I could see out across the black surface of Port Phillip. Back in 1892, fifteen local footballers had succumbed to those wintry waters. The players, from Mornington Football Club, were returning from a game against Mordialloc when their boat capsized at Pelican Reef. There were rumours they were drunk. Some of the players had stripped off to try to stay afloat. The cold water killed them. Their bones were still on the seabed, a few hundred metres from where I was now standing, stripped off, drunk and determined to finish my poem.

'… If you wanna get loaded, why don't you just order a shot? Bar's open.'

Below me, the pool flashed icy silver. I let myself topple, into a headlong dive. I wanted the cold shock. The noise of the strangers rose as I went. My breath was lost but I pushed myself deeper. I wanted to stay under for as long I could without dying. It seemed like a good place to hide. When I gave in, bursting back to the surface, Adam had a towel for me.

'We'd better get going,' he said.

'Back to the pub?' I spluttered.

'It's three o'clock in the fuckin' morning, mate,' he said. 'Pubs are closed. You need to go home. Enough's enough.'

23

Sweet Spots

By the middle of 1993, I had an established pub routine. My night was divided into stages. After making it past the bouncers with my fake ID, I leaned on the bar, drained pots and watched girls dance, waiting for the Dutch courage to kick in.

This was the alcohol-soaked sweet spot; the part I loved. The music, smoke, voices and colours were alive. My senses were tripping over each other. I guess I felt high. I didn't know any other drug that could do that for me. I'd had a couple of pulls of a homemade bong but all that gave me was a sickening coughing fit. I never did it again. Drink was my drug of choice.

There must have been a thousand local kids and young adults in the pubs every Saturday night. I knew all their faces and a lot of their names. Adam and I usually stayed close to each other, moving around during the night, from pub to pub, shouting over the music, perving at the girls, wondering if there were any of them who might be willing to kiss us, and laughing at ourselves. Every weekend felt like New Year's Eve.

In the sweet spot, I was good company. I was friendly and funny; maybe even charismatic. I knew I should have tried to make this stage of the night last longer by taking smaller sips. But

I was a big gulper. I couldn't help myself. If someone suggested skulling, I'd say 'Me first!' I only had one speed: flat out. I never wanted to stop.

Then came the next stage. I hit the dance floor.

In Funkytown, the late night place to go was the 21st Century Dance Club. It had a big neon sign and an even bigger reputation. We called it the Two-One. People from all over the city knew this venue because it attracted famous music acts and had a revolving dance floor, like one of those roundabout rides in local parks, only with smoke machines and throbbing music.

Even with a skinful, I was self-conscious under the disco ball reflections, just like I was back in primary school at the Blue Light Disco. My flat-footedness and stiff-hippedness was still an embarrassment. The most popular disco song in 1992 and 1993 was *Rhythm is a Dancer*. The DJ played it over and over. It taunted and haunted me. With no rhythm, I could never be a dancer. The only time I ever felt a hint of swagger on the dance floor was when I got to do 'Nutbush City Limits'. 'Grouse!' At the end of each cycle of prescribed moves, I dipped down to the floor for some extra flair.

Next door was the Pier Hotel, which had an upstairs bar called The Pink Pelican – or The Pelly. This was the smallest of the pubs. I used to go in there because it had a back door to The Two-One (the front door 21st Century bouncers were the hardest to get past). One night I stayed in The Pelly and got stuck into the spirits. There was a male strip contest on stage, so I went in it. I made the final but got beaten by some surfy dude with an amazing six-pack and long, blond hair. Our prizes were silky boxer shorts with cartoon characters on them. I wore mine every weekend for the next few months. Silk boxers felt like another way I could pretend to be a man ahead of time.

Others my age drank similarly but knew how to slow down as the nights drew on. I only became more disorderly, obnoxious and arrogant. Staring at girls became leering. Dancing became stumbling. Spewing up became inevitable. My unhalting drinking had everything to do with my insecurities around girls. When I was young, it was washing my mouth out with soap. Now it was a different type of cleansing. And I didn't just want to lose my shameful shyness, I wanted to obliterate it. Being out of control felt right and good, at least in the beginning.

I envied friends like Adam, Juan and Leo, who chatted to girls with obvious ease. Alongside them, I felt like a stupid animal. Drinking seemed like my only way to join in. But while my mates were downing drinks and standing firm, I was inevitably tumbling down a hill. The only way to stop was to hit the bottom.

It didn't help that my broader circle of friends found my drunken state amusing. I became increasingly loud and bold. I put people down. I pretended to be aggressive. Hilarious stuff. Adam never liked this side of me, but others seemed to. It became an expectation that I would play this role. So, I did, over and over again.

No girls found this version of me impressive, mind you. I was still a boy, but I was old enough to realise that the reason I drank so heavily was the also reason I could never find love in Funkytown on these wild nights.

I'd become a pisshead.

24

The Killer Returns

It was six o'clock on a bone-cold Thursday night in July. The streetlights had just blinked on. A train arrived at Seaford station, making the usual racket, loud enough to mute the dinging of boom gates at the crossing. The carriages slowed and jolted to a stop. The train exhaled dozens of city workers onto the platform. Most of them headed for parked cars. Headlights flared and engines revved but soon the taillights shrank into side streets and up towards the highway. The train moved on, bound for Kananook then Frankston, the end of the line.

Only a few of the commuters lived close enough to the station that they might choose to walk home. One of them was a woman in her forties, a bank clerk. She had long, dark hair and olive skin. It was only a five-minute walk to her house. Then she'd be out of the cold. She knew her son was waiting for her and they would soon be eating dinner together in their small dining room.

The woman crossed the road at the traffic lights and headed north along Railway Parade thinking she was alone. She went past the deserted Uniting Church, where my brother and I had once gone to Sunday school. The A-framed building had since been overgrown by bushes. There was a small sign with a picture of a red dove above a white cross, without which you wouldn't know it as a place of worship.

The woman followed the footpath beneath the low-slung power lines and wooden light poles, her shadow lengthening and shortening with each step. To her right were the orange-brick social rooms of the local soccer club, beside vast, vacuous playing fields, and three long car parks flecked with the glass of smashed beer bottles. On the other side of the road was a wall of tea-tree, roots like the gnarled fingers of old men, reaching into the gutter. On the other side of the tea-tree, between the road and Kananook Creek, was an abandoned railway building we all knew was used by drug addicts and the homeless.

All suburbs have pockets of isolation. This was one of ours. The woman was a couple of minutes from home when she drew level with a block of public toilets, under a large oak tree. I liked the seasonal grandeur of our suburb's oaks. In spring and summer, the breeze shook their leaves and made the sound of a healthy river. But on wintry nights like this, with the branches stripped bare, they were ominous.

Near the toilets, a man in an Adidas baseball cap was waiting, unseen. He carried a home-made knife and a fake gun. He started following the woman. She saw him about twenty metres away. She kept going, pretending not to be alarmed. Behind them, another train arrived, another flurry of traffic came and went. The man closed in. He grabbed the woman and tried to drag her back to the toilet block. She shrieked, resisting with all her strength. They fell down on the nature strip. Thinking he might want money, the woman offered her attacker her expensive ring. He refused it while straddling her on the wet grass. She felt the sodden earth beneath her skull. Her future vanished. Time had turned ruthless. From where she lay, she had only minutes, maybe seconds, left to live. She screamed for help. But the only person within earshot was a boy on a bike. He passed on the footpath, close enough to see the woman struggle. The kid thought it was a boyfriend beating his girlfriend. He kept riding, glancing back as he went.

The woman screamed again.

The killer spoke to her for the first time, warning her to be quiet, trying to cover her mouth. The woman stared into her attacker's face. She saw how young he was, with chubby cheeks and blue eyes. She bit his hand as hard she could. Through a grimace he said he had a gun. He pressed something against her temple. But she could feel it wasn't metal. It felt like wood. A fake gun? She'd take the risk. She twisted and bucked, breaking the killer's hold. As a car approached, she lunged towards the glow of the headlights, but the man seized her by her head, hard enough to reef hair from her scalp. She screamed again, but another train was passing behind the tea-tree and she was muted like the boom gates. Rattled by the woman's fight, the killer tried again to subdue her with the fake gun. More headlights. Again, the woman tried to scramble for the road. This time it worked. The driver saw her and stopped his car. She was saved. The killer fled like a startled bear, back towards the darkness of the soccer fields.

The driver took the woman home. Her son called Frankston police. Officers went, batons drawn, into the toilet block beside the soccer fields but found no trace of the man. At first the cops thought the attacker was just another mugger. They would soon discover just how wrong they were.

While police searched the toilets in vain, the woman's attacker walked back to Seaford station. He caught a Frankston-bound train to Kananook station, where Sarah MacDiarmid went missing, presumed murdered, three years earlier.

From Kananook station, he walked across Wells Road. Four blocks east, outside an old-style neighbourhood milk bar, he watched a woman park her Nissan Pulsar and go into the shop. He hurried over to the unlocked Pulsar and helped himself to the back seat. When the woman returned carrying some milk, he ducked out of view to lay in wait.

The woman's name was Debbie Fream. She lived nearby with her partner Garry Blair and their baby Jake, who was just twelve days old. When Debbie didn't come home from the shops, Garry and a friend organised a babysitter and went searching. Debbie and her car were nowhere to be found.

Life in Seaford changed forever that weekend. No one who lived among us could ever be the same. There was a time when I thought we lived in the loveliest place on earth. The murder of Elizabeth Stevens had changed that. With the disappearance of Debbie Fream, front-page news stories turned a harsh new light on the place I knew as Funkytown. They bristled with words like horror, terror and fright. My whole world felt different. I suspected my childhood was over.

part two

25

Night Rider

———————

When we were little, our family car was a beige Holden Kingswood HT. We just called it The Kingswood. We were aware that there were Holden families and Ford families, and that we were part of the Holden mob. Dad was no revhead. None of us ever watched Bathurst on television. There really was no reason to cling to this custom, but we did.

On our annual driving holidays to Sydney to see Dad's family, Jo would sit between my parents on the front bench seat while Steve, Kate and I sat in the back. We got to see Nana Kennedy and ride the Manly ferry and keep constant watch for funnel web spiders, which were apparently everywhere up there. My father was never happier than when he was back in his home city. He smiled so wide his moustache stretched horizontal from cheek to cheek. I'll never forget the way his fingers bounced along with excitement as he worked the three-on-the-tree gears of The Kingswood up the Hume Highway.

I came to love that car for the places it took us. I wanted my first car to be a Holden. Jo and Steve must have felt the same because their first cars were second-hand Commodores. Steve's was a bit fancier. It was lowered, with a V8 motor, and flash rims.

One night in June, I stole it. I was two months shy of my eighteenth birthday, so it was against the law for me to drive without an instructor, but I figured I was only going for a spin around the block. Steve must have been at his girlfriend's house. I was surprised he left his keys where I could find them.

At about ten o'clock, after Mum and Dad went to bed, I crept out of the house, unlocked the Club Lock steering wheel brace, and turned the key just enough to shift the column into neutral. Fearing that if I started the engine in the driveway I might wake my parents, I used all my strength to push the Commodore out onto the street.

I knew how to drive. Dad had been giving me lessons in the Hi-Ace van – it wasn't a Holden, but it also wasn't a Ford. I'd been behind the wheel on most of the highways and freeways of Melbourne. One Sunday afternoon, Dad had even let me drive all the way to Geelong to watch a golf pro-am. The tournament wasn't the point of our journey. It was a chance to hit the open road and talk. I asked most of the questions, probing Dad about his childhood, searching for pieces of me. I enjoyed his driving lessons. My older siblings said he could be impatient and grumpy as an instructor, but I didn't see that side of him. As long as I didn't go over the speed limit, he was fine.

The engine of Steve's car growled at first and then settled into a deep hum, as I eased off down our street. It was a different experience to driving the van. I felt too low to the ground, as if the body of the car was about to start scraping along the road. It was like driving an oversized go-kart. My plan to go around the block changed when I sensed the thrilling freedom of motion, the power of the V8. I decided to cruise to Frankston. That's when I saw the cops, lined up along the middle of the road. One of them was waving for me to stop. The car was an automatic so at least I didn't have to worry about going down through the gears. I slowed carefully and stopped beside a policewoman. I wound down my window, the freezing air slapping me in the face.

'Random breath test,' she said, looking at Steve's P-plate in the windscreen. 'Where you off to?'

'Just going to my girlfriend's house.'

'Okay, blow into this. One long breath.'

My pulse raced. I tried to appear casual; then I wondered whether I was being too nonchalant. For a moment, I forgot to breathe. My heart thumped away, matching the thrum of the motor. Could she tell I was driving illegally? She didn't seem suspicious. Was it a trap? I sucked in the air and exhaled into the plastic tube. I made a silent promise to go straight home if I got out of this without being charged with unlicensed driving.

'Where's she live?' said the copper.

'Frankston,' I said. Then my nerves got me rambling. 'Can't wait to get there, she'll have the heater on in her room. It's cold out here. Aren't you cold?'

The policewoman didn't answer. She looked me over one more time. My smile was slipping fast. Finally, she gave a wave. 'Keep driving. Have a good night.'

The engine rumbled again as I accelerated. Suddenly the Commodore's noise seemed too loud, as if it were calling attention to the police that I was getting away. There were other young-looking officers lined up on the edge of the road behind the booze bus. They studied me through the windscreen. Rather than avoid eye contact and risk looking dubious, I gave them a glance and a tremulous one-finger wave. They looked cold and bored as I rolled past. My vow to go straight home was forgotten as soon as I was in the clear. Fear fell away but my adrenaline remained, surging with the relief of not being busted. Heading onto the Frankston freeway, northbound, I put my foot down. I left the window open, let the wind sting my face. I wondered how far I could drive and where I might get to if I kept going until morning. I told myself that this was what it felt like to be grown-up. No shackles. No plans. No limits. I pushed the speedo needle to one twenty kilometres an hour, backed it off. Then I made another promise to myself to go home. This was one promise I would keep.

26

The Call

By July some of my Stingrays teammates were getting invitations to play in the AFL reserves competition. With the national draft only a few months away, recruiters' notepads were filling up. Smithy had already become a regular with the Sydney Swans. Brett Anthony was now there too. Benny Delarue was playing for St Kilda, and Dean Watson for Essendon.

After missing out on the Victorian match at the MCG, I didn't expect a call-up. I tried to stay hopeful, but the fear of failure crept in. Maybe I'd been kidding myself all along. Maybe I just wasn't good enough. Not daring to speak my fears out loud, I poured them into my journal.

Then, on a cold and dreary Thursday night, the phone rang at our house.

'Can someone get that?' Mum shouted from her bedroom. Dad was reading an old book in the backroom. He was going through a Henry Lawson phase.

Kate and I were in the lounge, entranced by the blaring wall heater and the latest episode of *Northern Exposure*. Thursday nights were good on telly.

'Anyone?' Mum said, before resorting to sarcasm. 'Don't

worry, stay where you are. I'll get it.'

A few seconds later, she stuck her head in the lounge to tell me my coach was on the phone. 'Hurry up.'

Hutchy had never called the house before.

'G'day mate,' he said. He sounded cheery. I tamped down my excitement. Maybe it was just a quick word about our game this weekend.

'Listen,' he said, 'you won't be playing for us this week.'

Oh no. I'd got it wrong. He was going to drop me from the side.

'Why not?'

'St Kilda needs an extra player and we've nominated you to have a go. They're playing Melbourne at Waverley.'

'You're kidding!?'

'No, are you keen?' Hutchy said.

'Shit yeah, grouse.'

I'd been wrong to be so glum about the Victorian game. I felt stupid and happy and relieved. And I was all-of-a-sudden nervous.

Hutchy congratulated me and I tore off to tell Mum and Dad. I wanted to tell Steve too, but he was still at training. Instead, I sprinted around to the Ray house to tell Adam. I didn't want to ride my bike. I wanted to feel my feet hitting the ground. The streets were empty. The estate was as quiet as the day we moved in fifteen years earlier. My breath was a burst of fog.

Adam opened the door to me ranting about Hutchy's phone call.

'Fuck, that's great,' he said. 'That's seriously a dream come true.'

Adam was as thrilled as I was. Fleeting envy might have occasionally been part of our relationship over the years, but never jealousy.

He shouted the news to his parents. From somewhere inside, Mr and Mrs Ray called out good luck.

'I'm just a fill-in for the week,' I noted.

'Don't talk yourself down,' Adam said. 'You've trained really hard for this chance. Show 'em what you can do. You can make it.'

I was taken aback. It had never occurred to me that Adam might be measuring my chances of success. Hearing this meant the world to me.

Adam's grin shifted to a thoughtful frown. 'It's so great you're chasing your dream. I've got to get off me arse and get amongst it. Join another band.'

'Sorry mate, I didn't come round to brag,' I said. 'You should do it.' He was jamming with some kids from school in a garage band. 'You should be playing to crowds.'

'Yeah.' He stared out onto the intersection of East and Downs roads, as if he were searching for someone. 'I'll do something.'

'We'll both make it,' I said. 'We'll both be famous.'

He turned back to me; grin restored.

We shook on it.

That night the streets of our estate, once a vast kingdom, felt too small. Those nights were becoming more common.

I ran all the way home, quickening my pace. It was like my legs were in charge of me and wouldn't stop. It was the same feeling of weightlessness I had at the Stingray Olympics at the beach in summer, only this was more powerful. I felt supercharged as I bolted past each house. I knew that behind those glowing curtains there were people who didn't know or care what was happening to me. I felt a ridiculous pity for their lot. They were going nowhere and I was out here, going at full tilt.

27

A Saint

―――――――――

Two days after my call-up, Mum and Dad drove me to Waverley Park to play for St Kilda. Sticking with tradition, I sat in the back of the van listening to Marc Cohn, biting down on my mouthguard, breathing in and out my nose, wiggling my toes.

Dad was euphoric that he didn't have to look for a spot in the crowded public car park off Jacksons Road. Players and their families were allowed to park in the members' area.

'Here we go,' he said, turning off Wellington Road.

It seemed like a milestone moment. I stopped the music and we enjoyed our arrival together.

'Good to see how the other half lives,' Mum said.

We hadn't been inside the members' car park since my bike-winning Little League game.

An attendant in a blue coat stopped us at the gate. Dad wound down his window. 'We've got one of the players here, mate.' His pride in making this announcement was contagious. I caught myself grinning.

The attendant looked through the window at me. 'Who ya playing for?'

'The Saints,' Mum said, beating me to it.

'Yeah, Saints,' I said.

'Good luck, champ.' He waved us through.

It was late morning. *Football Record* sellers were just getting set up outside the ticket offices.

'Rec-ORD, Rec-ORD.'

Dad bought one and gave it me. On the cover was a picture of Footscray star Doug Hawkins celebrating his three-hundredth game from the week before. I flicked to the team lists to find my name. It wasn't there; must've been printed before I got called up.

I said goodbye to my parents with a kiss for Mum and a handshake for Dad. They went to find a seat in the stands while I went looking for the change rooms. My heart pounded as I stepped inside. The other St Kilda players were pulling on socks and shorts and jumpers. Some were on the trainers' tables, getting strapped or massaged. My arrival was barely noticed. I wasn't sure if that was good or bad. Either way, I was terrified of not fitting in. There were the same noises and smells I was used to, only the blokes were hairier and bigger, some of them enormous. I hadn't been this close to adult footballers since my early days watching Seaford Football Club games. During the breaks, I used to edge as close as I dared to the tattooed giants. I looked up at them cursing, smoking, spitting and blowing snot on the grass. Now I had my chance to be one of them, on a whole new level.

My fear of being out of place was so overwhelming that I hadn't thought about the game itself. If this were a Stingrays match, I would have been imagining playing. Stomach churning, I would have been planning my traditional trip to the toilets. Instead, I was pre-occupied to the point of numbness. I needed those butterflies. They gave me the nervous energy that got me going. But they were nowhere to be found in that cavernous change room, and I couldn't conjure them.

Finding a locker for my bag, I sat down and tried to talk myself into belonging. Physically, I was a match for more than half the men in the room. I was one hundred and eighty-five centimetres and close to ninety kilos. I was as quick as anyone here, or nearly, and though I lacked big-game experience, I could mark, pass and tackle well enough to get by.

'C'mon,' I told myself. 'Snap out of it. Stand tall, stick your chest out.' I glanced round the room again, afraid the others might be judging me and my mutterings. Nobody seemed to notice a thing.

A voice by my side made me startle.

'Are you Paul Kennedy?' A property steward was standing over me. I nodded. 'Welcome mate, good luck. Here's your gear. That's the coach over there. He'll say g'day at some point.'

I took stock of the uniform. Brand new socks, arse-hugging second-hand shorts, and a slim fitting guernsey. I turned the jumper over to see what number I was: sixty. I didn't know numbers went that high.

While I got dressed, I studied the faces in the room. Some were smiling. The mood seemed relaxed, almost nonchalant – nowhere near as intense as teenage teams. I even detected some disinterest in the body language of older players. I recognised some of my teammates from TV. There was John Georgiou. He was even younger than me but had made his senior debut for St Kilda at sixteen. I used to play cricket against him. He hit the ball so hard that you hoped it wouldn't come your way. There was the ruckman Peter Everitt, nicknamed 'Spida'. He was as tall as any footballer I'd seen up close.

Some of the players started short, sharp kick-to-kick drills. Balls were thudding off boots, slapping into hands, giving the place a heartbeat.

The coach, Peter Francis, a former Carlton premiership player, gave me a warm greeting. I wasn't surprised to hear I'd be starting on the bench. I knew that if no one got injured I could be sitting on the pine for a half or more. I secretly prayed to my non-existent God for a couple of St Kilda hamstring injuries.

While Peter was talking to me, another player joined us. I was pleased to see it was Ant Harvey, brother of my hero Robert – the same Ant who'd berated me for staying out and drinking the night before a game.

'You two know each other?' Peter said.

'Yeah,' I said. 'Both Seaford boys.'

The coach left us to it.

'I heard you were playing,' Ant said, beaming. 'That's great.'

Ant had been recruited to the AFL in the mid-year draft. His climb up the ranks might have seemed inevitable considering he was the sibling of one of the best ruck-rovers in the country. But he wasn't as big as Robert, and he had to prove his worth in the Saints Under 19s, then in Frankston's Victorian Football Association (VFA) team.

'How have you been going?' I asked. 'Won't be long before you're up with Bob?'

'We'll see,' he said. 'I'm just enjoying it. The skills are sensational at this level. If you make space, someone will hit you on the chest. When you get out there, just keep running.'

When I mentioned to Ant that a few of our teammates looked

a bit bored, he nodded knowingly.

'Yeah, cause they're in the twos,' he said. 'They're pissed off they're not in the senior side.'

I hadn't stopped to think that this might be a depressing place for some footballers. There were three types of AFL reserves players: the rookie on the rise, the veteran on the slide, and the middleman who thought he had what it took to go all the way but was finding it harder than he had imagined.

'Did they tell you what position you're in?' Ant asked.

'David Dench,' I replied, invoking the name of North Melbourne's champion full-back as rhyming slang for the bench.

'Don't worry,' he said. 'You'll get on. Remember, it's just another game.'

In his pre-game speech, the coach pointed out that our opponent, Melbourne, was the top team, which meant that we had a chance to test ourselves against the best. Our team had apparently lost to Fitzroy the previous week by four points, and we didn't want to let another one slip. I wasn't listening too closely. I was trying to summon those elusive butterflies – imagining myself on the field, taking marks and dodging opponents.

'Time to get out there,' a voice shouted.

St Kilda's senior coach Ken Sheldon and a few of the firsts players were leaning against the walls as we went. There was Danny Frawley, Nathan Burke and Robert Harvey himself. The great man greeted me as I headed out. I could only manage a nod, and an earnest bite down on my mouthguard.

Waverley Park had always seemed vast to me, but today it seemed the size of two ovals. The members' wing went on forever. I couldn't even see the outer wing because of the rise and fall of the ground. The warm-up was a jog around the centre square. I couldn't take my eyes off the grandstands the whole time. There were enough early-bird barrackers to suggest a decent crowd was on the way. Already, I'd forgotten Ant's just-another-game advice. My attention kept straying to the occasion, rather than the match. I'm here! I can't believe it!

On the bench, I wore a black Hugh Hefner-style dressing gown to keep warm.

I sat there for what felt like an eternity. Just after half time, the coach made the call from his box high above me in the members' stand. The runner answered the phone next to us.

'It's for you,' he said, handing me the receiver.

I didn't know what to say. Throughout the first half, I'd seen other players being handed the phone as they came and went. Grunting seemed to be the preferred parlance. The more seasoned players answered with a breathless impatience. 'Yeah, yeah, all right.'

I didn't have the experience to grunt or give the coach any attitude. As politely as I could, I said, 'Hello?'

The runner smirked.

'You're on the wing, mate,' the coach said. 'On Greg Healy. Number thirty-three.' Then I heard a click.

I didn't need to be told Greg Healy's number. He was a former captain of the Melbourne Football Club. He'd played his best footy in the 1980s but in my eyes, he was still a star. His brother was Gerard Healy, the Brownlow Medal winner from 1988. Gerard had even attended a Stingrays training session at Hutchy's request. He was one of the most commanding men I'd ever seen.

Charging onto the ground, I spotted Greg Healy running near

the centre circle. I rubbed my shoulder against his to let him know I was his new opponent. He kept jogging as if I didn't exist.

Healy was bigger than I thought, with thick legs and a muscular neck. I stuck close, ready to pounce if he took possession. He didn't seem to be running too hard. I kept up with him okay most of the time. My contribution other than to watch out for Healy was negligible. A couple of times I rushed into space and called for the ball, but no one passed it to me. I managed to scavenge a couple of handballs. The pace of the game was manageable, and I could read the flow of the contest. But something was off. I felt like an extra on a movie set. In the Stingrays' team I was an important player; one of Hutchy's trusted regulars. In this team, I felt redundant. This, of course, was nobody's fault but mine. No one on the St Kilda side was excluding me. I just wasn't imposing enough. As Dad used to say when he was coaching me in the Under 12s, 'No one has any more right to the ball than anyone else. If you want it, go and get it.'

At the three-quarter time break, I wiggled my toes, pictured my favourite imaginary beach and breathed deeply.

In the last quarter, I ran harder, got to more contests and, belatedly, started to feel up to the challenge. It helped that our team was in front. Spida Everitt was dominating the ruck. Another regular senior player, Brett Bowey, was on fire. He drop-punted the ball as sweetly as anyone I'd played with. His foot connected with the ball like a one-wood off the tee.

Daring to leave Healy and go after possessions myself, I roamed the wing and flanks, willing the ball my way. When Bowey, with perfect balance, kicked diagonally across the field, it was my mate Ant who was fed the next handball. I started screaming for him to pass it to me. Ant sent a perfect lofted pass in my direction. I barely had to move. This was my chance. There was nothing between me and the crowd but a huge, empty wing. The only problem was I had too much time to think about what I was going to do next. I forgot to watch the ball.

It hit my chest, fell through my arms and dropped between my legs. As far as I could recall, I'd never dropped a chest mark in all my playing days – not even in the Under 9s. But I had now. I heard a collective groan from the crowd, with some mocking laughter. It was the sound you hear from your mates when a seagull shits on your head. By the time I reached to pick up the ball, I was swamped. Players piled in around me. A brief wrestle, then the umpire blew his whistle. 'Give it to me, I'll ball it up.'

The game ended soon after. That dropped mark would forever replay itself in my head, like a dodgy VHS tape: spilled mark, broken frame, spilled mark, broken frame. After the match I found Mum and Dad and we watched St Kilda's seniors get thrashed by the Demons. Best on ground was the Irishman Jim Stynes, who Hutchy had coached a few years earlier at Prahran, in the VFA.

With none of Waverley Park's notoriously muddy, post-game traffic snarls to contend with, Dad had us out of the members' car park in no time. It was a quiet ride home. Cutting through Dandenong on the way back to Seaford, Mum broke the silence to tell me how much she had enjoyed watching me play on the big stage. 'Hopefully, you'll get another go.'

28

Another Chance

Sure enough, a week later, I was back on the bench in the same thigh-high dressing gown as before. I'd been given one more chance to prove myself in the AFL reserves. Only this time, we were playing Carlton at Princes Park, on the other side of the city.

The coach had sent me on in the first half, but I'd copped an almighty whack in the nose. I staggered off the field, unable to see through my watering eyes. I was bleeding from my lip, from my nose and, as far as I could tell, back inside my skull as well. I didn't mind tasting fresh blood during a game; it was usually a prize for commitment to a collision. But this time it was just my own clumsiness – I'd got my head in the way of someone's forearm.

'It's stopped, I reckon,' the kindly trainer said, checking the cotton balls stuffed up both nostrils. He said my nose was probably busted, but there was nothing I could do about it now.

I shrugged. 'I already broke it a month or so ago,' I said. A stray elbow had crashed into my face in the Stingrays game against Eastern Ranges. Checking it out in the mirror at home, I'd noticed a small lump on the bridge. It hadn't gone away.

The trainer said he could tape my head to keep the cotton balls in. This sounded ridiculous, but I was desperate to get back out there. I was trying not to think about the fact that for the second consecutive week, I'd arrived at the ground without the familiar pre-game butterflies. Nothing was churning the way I wanted it to. But I had to push through it. I had plenty to prove.

The trainer unfurled a roll of tape and tied it around my head like a tennis headband, only it was secured under my snout. It felt stupid. Worse, I could only breathe through my mouth, which wasn't easy with a mouthguard.

'Howzat?' the trainer said. 'It might not be too comfortable.'

'Arrrgh ... yeah, okay,' I said. It wasn't my nose that was making me wince; it was the thought of not being able to make amends for my humiliation the week before. I was angry at myself for getting hurt. 'I'm fine.'

I took off the gown as a statement of my readiness. With a raised thumb, the trainer indicated to the runner that I was fixed.

While the runner was on the phone to the coach, I stood twitching at the edge of the interchange bench. On the far side of the oval, the Princes Park grandstand loomed like a wave in perfect barrel formation. The seats in the upper level were sectioned into bright coloured blocks. Blue. Red. Yellow. Green. It looked like a Rubik's cube. Then I saw there were plenty of people sitting in it, mainly in the lower level, near the fence. They were waiting for the senior game to start. Carlton was scheduled to play against the Brisbane Bears.

'Hey mate.' It was the runner, still holding the phone. 'Ready to go? Coach wants you on the back flank.'

Soon I was bolting back onto the green expanse, not as big as Waverley, but still wide and free. A man in the crowd yelled, loud and clear: 'Look! It's the mummy.' Others laughed along.

I didn't look back. My eyes were on the movement of the ball at the other end of the field. 'Hey, number sixty! Ya look like a fuckin' dickhead.'

In frustration, I ripped away the tape round my head, taking a tuft of hair with it. I threw it on grass, along with the bloodied cotton balls. If I bled, I bled.

Determined to make up for lost time, I made up my mind to launch myself at the first contest I could find. I wanted to impose myself on the match, not be a spectator. When the ball was slewed my way by one of the Blues, I steadied myself and relaxed, eyeing an easy mark. The Sherrin travelled further than I'd anticipated; I shuffled backwards but it floated beyond my grasp. As I turned to chase it, my head crashed into a brick wall masquerading as a Carlton player's shoulder. For the second time in twenty minutes, I heard my nose crack; as loud as a cattleman's whip, echoing in my brain. The crowd groaned, as if a car had just ploughed into a cyclist. Crumpled on the grass, I felt for my mashed nose, surprised it wasn't gushing blood like before. I thought maybe I'd run out. I hurried to my feet. My eyes were clear enough. Play had gone on. I'd never even got a finger on the ball.

In the huddle at three-quarter time, I reached for a cup of cordial, wondering what I was still doing here. My anger had receded. I felt shameful pangs of self-pity.

The heaviness I'd felt in my legs the week before seemed worse this time around. I wondered if all the late-night parties and Kentucky feeds had started to diminish my fitness: softened my stomach and stolen the lightness from my breath. But the weight I was lugging was also emotional. During the week I'd spoken to the Stingrays general manager about my prospects. He was in charge of liaising with AFL clubs about potential recruits. He said he'd been speaking to a mate from St Kilda about my game against Melbourne at Waverley.

'He said you looked slow,' the manager said.

'Righto,' I said. 'Did you tell him I'm not?'

'Oh yeah, I told him, I was surprised he said that. Did you play a good game?'

'Not flash.'

'Oh, that's probably why then.'

'I'll prove him wrong this week,' I'd said.

Now, with only a quarter to go at Princes Park, I hadn't proved anything. And I wouldn't get a third chance. In truth, I was already imagining going back to play at Seaford Football Club. At least people knew me there. I could be a rising star and people would pat me on the back. I could get drunk with the boys after the game and go out any night I liked and everything would be easier. Maybe the dream of breaking into the AFL wasn't all I'd built it up to be. It wasn't worth it. I wasn't as fit as I needed to be. No one was passing me the ball. And I was sick with doubt and fear. But what would I tell people back in Seaford when they asked what went wrong? I could always say I didn't really try my hardest. There were a dozen excuses I could use. No one had to know the truth.

'You okay?' Ant Harvey was watching me with an expression of mild annoyance. He was red-cheeked, sweating, more exhaling than inhaling. He'd been our best player all afternoon.

'Yeah.' I tried to appear nonchalant, touching my sore nose.

'No, not that,' Ant said. 'You look like you don't wanna be here.'

I searched his face for a smile. He wasn't joking.

176

'This is your *chance*,' he said. 'Have a crack. Don't be scared.'

My instinct was to tell Ant to shut up; that I wasn't afraid. But he was right. His words embarrassed me with their naked honesty. I wanted to click my fingers and disappear. In a few words, he'd reduced me to the frightened little boy I was.

Don't be scared.

The only other person who'd spoken to me like that was Hutchy. In recent games for the Stingrays, he'd commented on my listlessness; nudging me with rhetorical questions. 'You up for this?' 'You feelin' okay?' They were like cattle prods to my ego.

'Shit yeah,' I'd said. He believed me because he wanted to.

With Ant waiting on a response from me, I had nowhere to go. Once again, he'd seen right through me. My eyes went searching beyond the huddle, to the spectators on the terraces. Men wearing beanies. Children with mullets. Women eating hot chips from little yellow and red buckets. I started watching the flags on the top of the scoreboard next to the Coke, CUB Carlton and 3UZ billboards.

Ant poked me in the midriff. 'Mate, you're just cruising around.'

It wasn't the accusation that wounded me; it was that it was Ant saying it, right here, on the footy field. A part of me wanted him to go easy on me. 'Come on, Ant,' I wanted to say. 'We're both Seaford boys. We're in this together. Gimme a break.'

But that would only have added to Ant's disappointment in me, and his exasperation hurt me far more than any broken nose. He didn't understand my half-heartedness. Sure, we'd grown up in the same postcode, but he hadn't accepted the indoctrination of the local footy culture. His independent spirit had set him apart.

On that ugly night outside The Grand hotel, when I busted my hand, Ant was among us. He chose not to trade punches. Instead, he performed a minor miracle – he went and found a taxi. It was Ant who helped save us from getting killed or maimed that night.

Now this 19-year-old Saint was at it again, trying to steer me in the right direction. 'They asked you to come and play for St Kilda for a reason,' he said, his voice softening. 'Because you're good. Show 'em. If the ball's there, you get it.'

I slapped Ant on the arm. 'Thanks mate,' I said.

He just nodded, and took a swig from a water bottle.

The coach read out our line-up for the last quarter. Surprisingly, I wasn't benched. I took my place in the backline for the final quarter. Waiting for the bounce, I pulled up my socks and admired the black, white and red hoops on my shins. I had a flashback to watching St Kilda players on muddy days at Moorabbin in the 1980s, when Dad used to take Steve and me to those wintry games.

If the ball's there, you get it.

I charged off the line of the square as Carlton took possession through a tall ruck-rover. He was running my way with both hands on the ball, as if he might handball. I wasn't waiting to find out. I heaved my right shoulder into his navy-blue jumper. His stomach took my force and his legs buckled as my arms clamped his torso like a pit bull's bite. The whistle blew and I knew it was my free kick for holding the ball. 'Thanks,' I said, taking it off him. I heard him trying to suck in the air that had escaped his body.

I'd almost forgotten the crunching satisfaction of a good tackle; the sound of an opponent moaning in pain; the mutual understanding that it could just as easily have happened to you. When I was thirteen, I'd snapped my collarbone in a game. Instead

178

of calling an ambulance, Dad drove me slowly to the hospital in his old Holden. When we went over the railway line at Frankston, I felt every bump reverberate through my body and into my shoulder. 'Go slower,' I'd pleaded. Dad said sorry, while chuckling to himself at the absurdity of his decision to drive me. He reached out his hand to touch my arm. 'Sorry, mate,' he said. 'Almost there.'

'Back off ya mark,' the umpire was saying. 'Your kick.'

The ball was finally mine. I ran my hands over it, turning it around and around. I looked down at its taut laces and little rubber valve. The familiarity of touch felt like an antidote to my self-doubt.

I went back and took my kick, which found its target. Just like that, I felt like I belonged. The next twenty minutes surpassed all my previous feats in football, modest as they were to that point. Under a grey sky, with a breeze at my back, I forgot about my opponent and chased the ball, like a dog after a frisbee. Luck ran my way and I started to take marks, receive handballs, and even shout directions to other Saints. Most importantly, I stopped overthinking. The flow of the game, which had seemed hectic and foreign to me before, was now as familiar as kicking drop punts at the lightpost outside our house in Emanuel Drive. I felt fresh and new and dynamic. It helped that Ant's advice was echoing in my head. With every possession my confidence surged. Words of encouragement from teammates were extra fuel. At one point I snatched up a loose ball in the back pocket and took off. My opponent came close to catching me. I heard him straining with effort. The boundary line was close, but I wasn't about to surrender to it. I veered away, back into space. There were teammates on the wing, but they seemed miles away. Now I heard voices from

the crowd. Carlton supporters. 'Get him.' 'How far!?' I hoped
the Blues player chasing me wasn't quick enough. I sidestepped
one last time, swerving back toward the boundary. Without time
to straighten up again, I guided the ball with my left hand onto
my left foot. It wasn't my natural side, but it felt natural now. I
lowered it on an angle, the way you do when you want to kick
a torpedo. This was almost arrogant. It's hard enough to kick a
torpedo on the run with your preferred foot. Luck winked at me.
The ball landed in the perfect spot – to the side of my laces – and
the ball covered the distance to my target at head height. I soaked
up the clapping from Saints supporters.

Before I even knew it was close, the final siren blew. Back in
the change rooms, a teammate whose name I didn't know sat next
to me and said, 'Mate, you were on fire out there.'

One of the coaching staff followed up with, 'Did you get stung
by a bee or something?'

He'd summed up my two-week AFL audition nicely. I'd
been impressive for about as long as it took for a skin irritation
to settle. There were no recruiters rushing over to whisper in my
ear, although I hoped they'd seen something in me. I made sure
to thank Ant for his kind, stern words. He would go on to make
his senior debut a year later, taking his place alongside his older
brother. He never stopped giving everything he had.

That night, I got rolling drunk with Adam and some other
mates at an eighteenth birthday party. Once again, I'd washed
Ant's advice away with beer and spirits.

We wandered home amid the whirr of hovering police
helicopters. I was too far gone to pay much attention, but a search
party had been launched earlier that day for Debbie Fream, the

Kananook mother who went missing after driving to her local shop.

While my mates and I sang and hollered in the empty streets, the rest of the community was facing up to the very real possibility that there was a serial killer in our midst. At first the searchers were just family and friends. Now it was choppers, homicide detectives, dog squad and State Emergency Service (SES) volunteers. The search for Debbie Fream had become desperate.

29

Bad Feeling

Debbie Fream's Nissan Pulsar was found a day after she disappeared. It was dented and dumped in a Seaford street. The driver's seat was pushed all the way back, as if a very tall person had been in it. Debbie Fream was not tall.

By Sunday, it was as if the entire Victoria Police force had arrived in our suburb. Line searches had been organised along the bay foreshore and the banks of Kananook Creek. They were already running out of places to look.

As if my hangover wasn't bad enough, my face was tender from the knocks I took at Princes Park. My legs ached. In the shower I guzzled the warm water until I vomited. That always made me feel better.

Shuffling into the living room, I decided it was a good day for watching movies. Luckily, I had a few spare coins left over from the night before.

Our local video shop had a full range of new releases and about six rows of weeklies. I reckon I wore footmarks in the carpet along the new release wall.

But with Mum waiting for me in the video shop car park this time around, I had to rush my pick. I came up with a movie called

The Prince of Tides. I liked Nick Nolte. I could take or leave Barbra Streisand.

On the way back home, Mum flicked to the news on the radio.

'Wonder if they found that woman,' she said flatly.

A police detective's tone answered Mum's question.

'There's been nothing of any substance from the search to date,' he said. He appealed for public help, gave details of the missing young mother, and talked about her baby son, Jake.

'Poor boy,' Mum said.

The detective also spoke about the missing woman's de facto partner, Garry Blair. There'd been photos of Garry in the newspapers, pleading for help. He was a skinny man, with a dark mullet haircut. In one picture, he was sitting in a cop-shop chair, arms crossed, stroking his thin moustache. You could feel his cold, panicked confusion.

The police got Garry to say a few words at a press conference. 'I'd like the public to really jog their memory,' he said. 'If they saw anything on Thursday night at approximately seven, seven-thirty – really think back to that time in the Seaford area – then contact police. No one can imagine the pain and agony of just sitting around waiting for a word. It's not like Debbie. What's gone wrong?'

Journalists asked him about baby Jake. 'He's doing all right,' he said. 'He's missing his mother. Just like me. But he's doing all right.'

Finally, we heard journalists asking whether this case was linked to other murders.

It chilled me to think we lived only a two-minute drive from where Debbie's car had been dumped. The milk bar where she was last seen was almost as close. This was real. It was happening right here. I wondered why I hadn't thought about it like that before. I knew by Mum's expression she was way ahead of me. Her eyes had softened at the news on the radio.

'Will they find her?' I asked.

Mum didn't answer straight away. She waited until we were turning into our driveway. 'Doesn't look good, mate,' she said. 'But we live in hope.'

That afternoon I cried watching Nolte and Streisand fall in love. The story broke my heart and put it back together again. Later, I would track down the book that inspired the film. Like Margaret Craven's novel, I read Pat Conroy's *The Prince of Tides* for enjoyment. It changed my view of the world, and of how I saw myself in it. The book was three times more mesmerising and devastating than the film. Conroy seized me with his opening lines: 'My wound is geography. It is also my anchorage, my port of call. I grew up slowly beside the tides and marshes of Colleton ...' He pulled me in closer to whisper his secrets about Tom Wingo, troubled English teacher and football coach. How could such a man be so gentle? Conroy taunted me with his mastery of words. His writing was art, as lovely as anything I'd seen or felt. I was honoured to turn his pages. His flourishes of language seeped into me and his truths threatened to tear me apart. When I reached the final page I called for him not to leave me.

As the credits rolled on the movie version, I was hauled back to reality. There was breaking news in the search for Debbie Fream. A farmer had found a woman's body in a paddock at Carrum Downs. It was a suburb away from where we lived, on the other side of the industrial area. To get to Carrum Downs from Kananook you had to pass through our estate. Is that what happened? Was she still alive when he took her this way?

Police confirmed that Debbie Fream had been murdered. Apparently, the farmer thought she was a mannequin lying there in the grass. There were ferns on top of the body. After an examination – scratches on her hands, no drag marks, no rape, stab wounds in her neck, strangle marks – police concluded she had been killed after trying to fight off a man with a knife.

Grief and fear descended on us that weekend. I began to imagine what kind of man was capable of such horror. I tried to think of a scenario where I might be able to catch the killer. Truth was, just thinking about him spooked me. My fear shamed me. This mongrel was killing girls and women, not boys and men. My relative safety, given I was male, brought me a sense of relief, guilt and helplessness. But one aspect of our predicament became universal: no one who breathed the same air as we did in that bleak winter could get into a car without checking the back seat. It became a habit that we talked about and shook our heads at.

I remember asking Dad what we could do. He raised his eyebrows in thought.

'Just try to be aware,' he said. 'When I go for a walk now, I keep an eye out and when I see a girl or woman, I make sure I cross the road so she can see me getting out of her way. Just to put her mind at ease.'

Soon he stopped going for walks altogether. Other men did the same. After dark, the streets all but emptied, as if there were a pandemic and no one wanted to catch the virus.

30

A Different Story

While the national media's attention was drawn to the prospect of a homicidal maniac on the loose in our streets, I tried to keep my mind on school. By day, at least. My mates and I were into our second semester of Year 12 and I'd got poor to modest marks on my mid-year assessments. My plans for a good VCE score were falling away by the day. I'd made promises in my diary to reinvent myself as the world's best student but, like my footy ambitions, those dreams had been replaced by heavy hangovers.

Though I wasn't admitting it to myself, I desperately needed something to steer me off the path to self-destruction. That something came my way in the form of a writing challenge. For English, I had to complete three short stories to get a pass. My ever-patient English teacher, Mrs Golden, urged me to write about anything other than football. This was a refrain from every English teacher I'd ever had. I wanted to please Mrs Golden – who once described me on one of my report cards as an 'exasperating student' – but time was running out. I decided I would give the short stories my all.

I began to pen a story about Dad as a boy, losing his father so suddenly. Imagining myself as that poor, devastated child,

I cried while I wrote it. At times the tears were unstoppable; I had to keep pausing between pages. I was grieving for the loss of my grandfather, who I never knew, and for my father, who should've been able to grow up with a dad. With a first draft complete, I surprised myself by going back over it three more times.

The next day I wanted to show my story to someone before I submitted it to Mrs Golden. At lunch, Adam and I swung past the small lounge office where Mrs Mac hung out with her best friend and fellow English teacher Mrs Regnier, who we called Mrs Reg.

We didn't bother knocking.

'G'day,' I said. 'Not interrupting?'

Mrs Mac and Mrs Reg both smiled. They were drinking coffee from black mugs.

They were the most bookish women I knew, though neither of them was the slightest bit uncool; in fact, the opposite was true. I regarded them with equal admiration, if not awe. They were different to most other teachers. I imagined they might've been easily bored by workplace politics or the usual grumblings in the staff room.

'To what do we owe this honour?' Mrs Reg asked.

'Good question,' Adam said. He was never rapt when I suggested we chew the fat with teachers. He never understood my need to bond with Mrs Mac and Mrs Reg. Nor did I. When I'd got sick with the measles the previous year, he thought it was weird that Mrs Mac and Mrs Reg asked him to pass on a get well card they'd written me. The card assigned me homework, including summarising 'the complete works of W Shakespeare.' It finished with: 'Get better soon. No one else appreciates our humour.'

I sat on a chair and put my feet on the nearest desk.

'Make yourself at home,' Mrs Reg said.

'Thanks. Hey, I've written a story for English,' I said to Mrs Mac. 'Do you mind reading it for me?'

'Sure, now?'

Suddenly I was all nerves; welcoming back the butterflies that had refused to show up before my footy games. 'Maybe I'll give it to you after class if that's all right.'

When Lit finished later that day, I waited until everyone had left the classroom before I handed Mrs Mac my story.

'You can take it away with you,' I urged.

Mrs Mac was having none of it. 'I'll read it now,' she said. 'What's it about?'

'My dad.'

I could feel my face flush red as Mrs Mac started reading it right in front of me. I paced the other side of the room, stealing glances at my teacher for any tell-tale reactions.

After several rewrites, I had settled on Dad dying the same way as his father did back in 1958. In the story, I was living without my hero and mentor. It was fiction with elements of truth about our relationship.

Mrs Mac was on the last page, in which I wished I could hug Dad one more time. She paused to touch the corner of her eye. She didn't lift her head, rather shifted her gaze above the paper to look at me.

'This is really lovely,' she said.

'Dad's not really dead,' I said. 'But that is how his dad died when he was a kid.'

Again, she dabbed at her eyes. 'You can be a good writer when you try.'

Mrs Mac handed me back the sheets of paper and I all but skipped out of the room. It only occurred to me later that she didn't ask why I made the decision to kill off my father. I was glad. It saved me thinking about the answer.

I showed the story to Dad a few days later. He was checking his Tattslotto numbers at the time. I left him alone to read it, but when I came back he said the story had got him crying. I'd never seen him cry, nor had I imagined it was possible.

'It's very good,' he said. 'It's very touching to read those lovely things you said about me. It means a lot.'

The pride I felt was tinged with regret. I realised now that it was a cruel thing to take away someone else's grief and toy with it for personal gain. I'd used Dad and his trauma to try and impress my teachers.

When my guilt drained away, however, I felt buoyed by the power to evoke an emotional response through words. The thought of Mrs Mac's response, of my father's tears, gave me the confidence to try again. For the first time, I started to fantasise about being a writer.

Not long after, Mrs Mac came to me with a suggestion: 'Have you ever thought about going into journalism?'

I told her I didn't want to be a reporter. I wanted to be a novelist. Like Conroy or Craven. I knew it was ridiculous. It was like saying you wanted to be Daicos without ever kicking a ball into the sky.

'Maybe you should,' Mrs Mac said. 'Margaret Craven started out as a journalist.'

31

Curfew

As the manhunt continued, people in Seaford, Frankston and the surrounding suburbs spent more time in their homes, trying to stay safe, waiting for updates from the Homicide Squad. Killer's curfew. Even the nightclub and pub crowds started to thin.

Emotionally, I could feel the community draw each other closer. While newspaper headlines were all about fear, there also was anger among locals. Police had arrived in impressive numbers – like an army battalion – setting up operations in Frankston and other local stations, but at the regular press conferences, commanders kept offering the same line that they were uncertain the same madman was responsible for killing both Elizabeth Stevens and Debbie Fream. I thought the police's hesitancy was nonsense, even if I understood why they were being careful with information.

I did my best to concentrate on my short-story assignment. Having submitted my story about Dad to Mrs Golden, I decided that for the other two I should stick to personal experience. I told the story about the fight outside The Grand. Then I moved on to a tale about a failed one-night stand from around the same time.

This one I gave to Mrs Mac. She said she liked it, but felt it lacked realism. She didn't believe I would have been honest with my mates about my sexual failure. She thought I should change it to a boastful lie. But I didn't want to. I explained to my teacher that while boys did bullshit each other a lot about their escapades, real mates tended to tell the truth when it came sex. At least, that's how it was with Adam and me. Mrs Mac seemed surprised. Perhaps she might've been wondering how someone who could pretend his father had died was so morally superior about upholding the rules of rooting banter.

My stories felt epic while I was writing them; like I was exhibiting some sort of long-dormant talent. Looking back, I realise they weren't particularly special. But they gave me the freedom to explore themes close to me. Heartbreak, violence, freedom, and untold futures. And my writing improved with each draft.

Finally, I felt I was on a roll at school.

32

Captain Seahorse

Around the same time, another favourite English teacher, Mr Casey, organised an interschool footy match for our senior team. 'Case' announced that we'd be playing a one-off game against John Paul College in Frankston.

Case loved his footy as much as I did. And he asked me if I'd captain the team.

'Bloody oath,' I said.

Game day was set for a Wednesday so it didn't clash with club footy. Hutchy must have kept his fingers crossed that none of his players got hurt in these school matches. The Stingrays were on a winning streak, finals bound, marching to the MCG.

Our school didn't own a bus, so Case hired one. On the way to meet up with the team in the school car park I happened to walk past Louise, who was standing with her books held against her chest like girls did in American movies. I was too high on pre-match excitement to feel awkward around her.

'Lou,' I said, so loudly I surprised both of us.

'Hello stranger,' she said. It was good to hear her voice. 'I saw Adam and the rest of your friends go out there.' She pointed out past the canteen to the path beside the gym. 'Footy today, hey?'

I smiled and so did she. Was she keen to talk or did she just want me to keep going to the bus? I could never read her body language. This was part of the reason I hadn't really talked to her since she dumped me. I'd developed a bat-like radar for her movements in the playground, and made sure I was always around mates – a natural shield against conversational invaders. Today, none of that mattered. I felt free standing with her. Her hair was tied back from her face, blue eyes sparkling. She was pretty as a long sunset. And she smelled nice.

'You look good,' I said, then got really bold. 'You always do.'

'Ta,' she said. 'You trying to grow your hair?'

'Yeah.' I pushed my hanging fringe across my forehead. 'I'm not cutting it for a year to see what it looks like.'

'I think you'll look good,' she said.

I wanted to reach out and touch her arm or shoulder, not lovingly, just to make contact. We made more small talk. I asked about her family and friends before changing the subject to her new boyfriend. It was a relief to have it out in the open. Louise gave a half smile. 'Who told you I had a boyfriend?'

'I saw you two at a party once,' I said. 'What was his name again?'

She told me his name, but I wilfully forgot it. I didn't know him. He went to another school, if he went to school at all.

'I don't know if it's serious or not,' she said. But I'd already seen her light up at his mention. She liked him more than she used to like me, I thought. I wasn't as jealous as I reckoned I'd be.

Coach Case hustled by holding his clipboard. With his helmet hair and thick glasses, he looked like he was off to a maths conference, not a game of footy. He had a bounce to his stride. I'd seen that elevated gait on Hutchy before Stingrays matches.

'About to leave mate,' Case said. 'Need to hurry.'

It broke the thrill of being close to Louise. She wished me luck.

I glanced back as I went, perhaps to remember Louise in that moment, that year, that time in my life. Her eyes shone like the sky. I was grateful to her for making things easier between us, and for everything else. For seeing past my bravado and liking me anyway. For holding me so close, if only for a short time. She had opened up something inside me that would never again be closed. In her eyes, I could see how possible it was for me to fall in love.

When our bus headed through the gates of John Paul College, I was clear minded and euphoric. My stomach started churning just like old times.

'Here we go, boys,' I said. The oval looked like a paddock without cows. There were no fences, no spectators. I was surprised to see goal posts. The home team was loitering on the sidelines, watching us pull up. I looked for the players I knew, including two of my best friends, Juan and Leo. We waved and grinned, my nervous energy settling into a state of complete contentment.

Juan came over to us, giving handshakes and half-hugs. 'You motherfuckers are goin' down.'

'Nah, cunt,' Leigh said, dry as a northerly wind. 'You are.' Leigh was a much talked-about local full-forward. He'd kicked a hundred goals for Seaford in the Under 15s. I thought he could've played professionally if he cared more about it.

Leo flicked his head back to say g'day. 'We're tagging ya,' he said to me.

Tagging had become a popular smothering tactic to stop a good opposition player from getting too many kicks and handballs.

'Won't matter to me,' I said. I was planning on being aggressive with anyone who came too close to me.

'All right boys, let's move it.' The instructions came from our co-coach, Mr Slater. He was a thick-chested fitness fanatic, a dead ringer for the Chesty Bonds singlet model, only with a black moustache. Like Case, he spoke to us in exclusively short sentences. 'Come get ya jumpers.'

We wore the old colours, red and green (from when our school went by another name: Seaford-Carrum High). There was a mix of no-sleeves and long-sleeves. Boys with contoured arms went sleeveless. The kids without gym memberships chose to cover their spindly limbs.

'These things stink,' Adam said, sniffing at the old wool. 'I reckon these've been worn by every school team since the seventies.'

The game started with a coin toss. I won it and picked an end to kick to.

Case had chosen Adam to play on the ball with me. He was a good footballer, even if he talked down his talent. A year earlier he'd represented St Kilda schoolboys in the Victorian Under 15s carnival. He played like he lived: tough, honest, and likely to crack a gag when the game was at its most serious, causing everyone to realise it was just a frolic.

Standing in the middle of the ground before the first bounce, Adam gave me a knowing smile.

'Wait for it,' he said, holding up a finger.

'For what?' I said.

A voice rose from the backline. 'Carn the fuckin' Seas!' one of our teammates howled, invoking our school emblem – a seahorse.

'And there it is,' Adam said. 'Classy.'

Away we went, chasing and kicking and tackling and dodging and puffing. The game was a perfect blend of competitiveness and joviality. John Paul had a Year 11 boy called George Harrack tagging me. I didn't know George, but I admired him immediately. He stuck to me like dirt on sweat, even after I roughed him up a bit. George would later play for the Stingrays and win the club best and fairest.

My personal highlight came deep in the first quarter. A John Paul player kicked out from the goal square. I anticipated he'd go wide to the outer flank. It was a well-timed kick, straight, with a Sydney Harbour Bridge-shaped arc. Senses sharp, I saw the ball turning end over end in slow motion and I knew I was going to mark it before I jumped onto my opponent's shoulder blade. I rose higher than I'd been before. The boy beneath me was strong, so he didn't crumple. It was as if we were practising hangers at lunchtime and he'd volunteered to be my stepladder. Muscle memory played its part; my next action felt instinctive, unrushed. I straightened my torso to give me extra height. At the last moment, I pushed off – almost jumping off my knees – propelled higher to take the ball in front of my eyes. The leather didn't budge in my hands. I brought the ball down, landing on my feet like a big cat.

The mark wasn't to be paid though. The umpire had blown his whistle for quarter time while the ball was in the air. I was so busy soaring I hadn't even heard it.

I didn't think I could feel as happy as I did after landing that speccy. I was wrong. Arriving at the team huddle to see my friends' faces was better. Doc put his long arm around my shoulder and gave my right ear its own personal woohoo. 'Sweet ride, man.'

'Fair leap,' Leigh said. 'Decent hangtime.'

The other boys slapped me on the back and I felt compelled to tell them it had been more arse than class.

Adam was shaking his head. 'We've been tryin' to do that at every fucking lunchtime for a year and you just come out here and do it in a game.'

The rest of the game went by too quickly. There was no scoreboard so no one cared too much about who was winning. In the last quarter I wanted to stop time. I wanted to stay on the field with Adam, Leigh, Doc and all the other boys forever. On the way home, we beamed with uncommon pride.

Later, someone told me the school was going to buy new jumpers – blue ones. The red and green was going to be retired with our catchcry. I was the last Captain Seahorse.

33

Speaking Out

_____

A packed-out public meeting to discuss the murder investigations was held at Seaford Community Hall on the banks of the Kananook Creek, a hundred metres from the dinging boom gates of the station crossing. Along with senior police, Melbourne's media bigwigs were there to broadcast it and write about it for the papers.

'How do we know the killer's not in the room with us now?' a woman asked.

'I'm very scared,' said another. 'I don't leave my home after five at night.'

'It's about time they brought back capital punishment,' a man said.

Applause followed this comment. With no breakthrough in sight, the killer was roaming our imaginations just as he was roaming our streets.

Police obfuscation, however well-intentioned, wasn't working. We weren't stupid for chrissake. Two of our own had been murdered. The crimes were all too similar. And there were others that might have been linked. What about Sarah MacDiarmid? What about other unsolved murders over the years? Could they all be the work of one lunatic? The meeting grew more and more emotional. Like a brooding, thick-toothed animal, anger is no good caged up.

The cops were on edge too. They called our collective suburban reaction to a serial killer's presence 'a siege or fortress mentality', as if it was wrong. I supposed the authorities' keep-calm attitude was as natural as our need to lash out.

The Mayor of Frankston, Denis Shaw, sided with his constituents. He said it was better to hang one innocent person than let convicted murderers back on the streets after a prison term to kill again. 'Even if he got fifteen years' jail, he could still come out and kill again, that's unjust,' he told his audience.

None of this helped inform us about the investigation. But it was obvious a discussion of revenge helped fend off an awful sense of helplessness. This type of gathering was practical and typical of the world I grew up in – adults speaking up without any overbearing hierarchy to adhere to. Even the mayor didn't seem to know he wasn't supposed to be part of the baying crowd.

Mum and Dad didn't want to go to the public meeting. As it was, there were far too many people to fit in the hall. But attendees did their best to squeeze in. Nobody wanted to be shut out in the chilling heart of this cruel winter. As a family, we all stayed at home that night, my siblings included. It was a strange thing to do; to watch on television from your loungeroom the happenings of our hometown. But it felt good to be together, and as normal as we could be.

Since Debbie Fream's body was found in the paddock, so many of us had changed the way we lived. Owners of shops and offices in Frankston had hired security guards to escort female workers to their cars after every shift. Security firms were run off their feet sending guards to private homes, to make sure they were secure.

I heard that some neighbours in pockets of Seaford and Frankston were chipping in money for security guards with Alsatians to patrol their streets. After all, the police couldn't be everywhere. Women rang the Peninsula Indoor Sports Centre, beside the old skating rink, and booked in for karate lessons. That sport hadn't been so popular since *Karate Kid* in 1984. Martial arts centres hired out their instructors to other sports clubs to shepherd women from social rooms to car parks. Husbands weren't happy with their wives walking to their cars on their own. All around us, the ominous words echoed: Don't go anywhere alone.

I asked Mum whether she was scared. She told me that as long as she was careful she knew she was fine. I supposed she was trying to protect me from too much worry. It worked. My mother had a knack for putting me at ease. I didn't ask other girls or women in my life how they felt about their personal safety. It was a dumb question. It seemed patronising because I knew I could never really understand their anxiety.

At the Seaford Community Hall meeting, police gave mixed messages, telling women not to walk the streets alone while also insisting people should continue with their daily lives.

Mayor Shaw was not impressed. 'It's appalling to say that – that women should be able to walk the streets without fear – but until this perpetrator is caught they shouldn't take that risk.'

As to the details of their investigation, finally detectives made the connection between the attack on a woman near Seaford station and Debbie Fream's murder. The woman who escaped with her life had given a sketch artist her description of the killer. A photofit was released. The suspect was twenty to twenty-five, about one hundred and eighty centimetres tall with a solid build and chubby face. The picture had the man wearing a beanie. He was clean-shaven, with small eyes and thin lips. His nose was the only feature that looked to fit his face.

Meanwhile, a profile of the suspect was being pieced together behind the scenes. The man in charge was Inspector Claude Minisini, a Melbourne-based officer who had studied at FBI headquarters in Virginia. Though his expertise was in sex crimes, and neither Elizabeth Stevens nor Debbie Fream were sexually assaulted, Minisini's experience in behavioural analytics was invaluable. After visiting the crime scenes, he theorised that the killer was a local, unemployed man (unable to hold down a job due to his murderous fantasies), aged between eighteen and twenty-four. He drew a triangle on a map to show the other detectives the small area in which he believed the killer operated. In the middle of the triangle was Kananook station in Seaford.

Time was a big factor in this profiling work. Inspector Minisini and his team were aware that this type of killer, who went out hunting when the bloodlust overtook him, was likely to strike again sooner rather than later. The high he felt from each crime would be less intense than the previous one. Unrestrained, the killer could become prolific in a hurry. Elizabeth Stevens was attacked on 11 June, Debbie Fream, 8 July – a twenty-six-day interval. By that grim measure, another attack was entirely possible before 3 August. Police began knocking on doors again, to find the killer they were convinced lived behind one of them.

34

Boys Fought

Though I grew up in the most peaceful of households and only ever knew love at home, violence was a familiar thread. I knew when it was coming, like a huntsman sensing a storm. I knew it the first time I fought. When I was ten, a kid nicknamed Skid challenged me on my way home from school with Adam. Skid looked underfed. But what I didn't know was that he could box. His punches were straight and sharp. I gave my best impression of a clothesline in a gale. Skid gave me a blood nose with one of his jabs. I consoled myself by claiming I won the fight. Adam agreed I'd been victorious, but we both knew Skid had my number. I felt I'd let Adam down by not living up to expectations of a tough friend.

Now we were older, we knew the risk was always there. Boys fought. Especially in Funkytown. On its worst days, Frankston could seem like Bartertown from *Mad Max Thunderdome*. Ten men enter, one man leaves.

Every time I went there as a teenager, I was conscious of the shape and unspoken aggression of other boys killing time by sizing each other up. I wasn't frightened of injury as much as humiliation. My greatest fear was that I might be beaten up in front of onlookers.

A day or so after the match against John Paul, Adam and I were walking through Frankston's shops, looking at everything and nothing. Usually, we'd be flat out rubber-necking at girls but there weren't many around to perv on. It was a grey, dull day. We sauntered past the cinema, which was offering a special deal of six-buck tickets, as if trying to entice people out of their homes. The big release at the time was *The Firm*, starring Tom Cruise. The promotional poster read: 'Power can be murder to resist.' The Hollywood hype paled in comparison to the banner headlines outside our newsagents: MURDER GRIPS FRANKSTON; THE FACE OF FEAR; NEIGHBOURHOOD IN GRIP OF TERROR.

Adam suggested we head back to the bus stop. 'Let's go home, there's nothing happening.'

'One more lap,' I said. 'Whatdaya reckon?'

'Righto.'

We walked through Quayside, the newest shopping centre; we meandered up and down the escalators outside Target, and up as far as Myer. While girls were scarce there were plenty of boys, schoolkids or otherwise. Ratbags, Dad would have called them. I clocked a few sideways glances. Sometimes there was eye-balling, which amounted to a test of nerves. Rational teenagers knew if you looked at an irrational kid the wrong way, you'd be challenged on it. These are-you-lookin'-at-me rituals posed no danger inside the shopping centres because of security guards, and the increased police presence.

Cops from all over Melbourne had been brought in for Operation Reassurance. A sign in the forecourt said the officers were there between eight o'clock in the morning and eleven o'clock at night to 'provide feedback and information'.

I guessed they were also there to look for anyone suspicious. No police ever spoke to us. Suppose we looked innocent enough. Adam was in his trendy jeans. I had my trusty tracky dacks on. We were both wearing surf-branded hoodies under warm jackets.

After a lap of the centre, I noticed a group of boys looking our way.

'Mate, they're starin' at us,' Adam said.

We recognised them as Frankston regulars. There were always four or five of them together. I never saw them smile. This meant they were serious about maintaining their image as bad arses. Their leader's name was Tremaine. He was muscular, with an unusually broad back, spiky hair, and black eyes under a thick brow. Tremaine was rumoured to have some sort of martial arts black belt. I assumed it was an urban myth. Adam used to tell kids he was 'a black belt'. Then he started telling people he was a 'sensei'. He wanted to see if the rumour caught on. It didn't.

Tremaine's second-in-charge was a boy called Riz, who was also in good physical shape. You could tell he lifted weights. Whenever I saw Riz, I took him to be agitated, with something to prove. He was a keen eye-baller.

'Don't worry about them,' I said.

We set a steady course through the shopping centre's automatic doors. I was relieved to be going home. We walked along a quiet laneway without looking back.

'Let's get out of this fuckin' place,' Adam said. I was pleased he felt the same way I did.

Our submissive walk-away gesture to the other boys might

have been a mistake, more likely it was inconsequential to what happened next.

As we came to the rear of the Peninsula Centre, beside the empty Quayside loading dock, Adam nudged my arm. He pointed straight ahead. In the reflection of an office window ahead of us I could see we were being followed.

'Fuckin' stop!'

Adam and I turned around. It was Riz talking.

'Where d'ya think you're going?'

They encircled us. I counted five. Riz stepped up, within striking distance, while Tremaine stood behind me. My pulse raced. My fingers were twitching. I lifted my hands to my chest ready to block or throw a right cross if necessary. One of the other three boys in the group, who I didn't recognise, was in my face. He was berating me. 'Havin' a crack at me mate's missus, were ya?'

'What?' My confusion was genuine. I didn't know who or what he was talking about.

The kid started ranting. He was small and thin-shouldered. He was accusing me of talking to his friend's ex-girlfriend outside the local footy club. I remembered the girl now. It was Cassie, my former primary school classmate with the pigtails, who I'd chatted to briefly after the players' revue.

'Whose girlfriend is she?' I said.

'She was mine,' said one of the other smaller boys.

'Was or is?' I said.

Adam spoke up. He knew the ex-boyfriend. They'd played a bit of footy together.

He explained we both knew the girl and there was nothing in it.

'Relax fellas, we don't want any trouble,' Adam said. I smiled at his calming voice, grateful as always that he was there. The shock of confrontation began easing. My heart settled back to its regular rhythm. I dropped my hands. I didn't even see the punch coming.

The blow to my jaw came from behind. Black lights flashed in my head. When I regained my senses, I was still standing in the same spot but my body was bent in half and I was clutching the side of my face. I heard slow echoes of cheering. All the world's colours were tinged grey. My sight was fuzzy. But things got clearer, like a camera finding focus.

Adam and I were moving up the street. We didn't run fast, our pace no quicker than a brisk walk. Our tormentors followed. Now they were taunting me.

I thought I knew one truth about hand-to-hand conflict. What you did was who you were. If you fled, you were cowardly. Not standing up to these boys felt wrong, but my overwhelming urge was to get out of harm's way.

Some part of my rattled brain rushed me back to the day Dad was confronted. We were at the MCG as a family, all six of us. I was about twelve. The game had finished. We were marching with the rest of the crowd down the stairs of the old grandstand when we encountered a dust-up between two twenty-something blokes. Both were scruffy, scrawny and pissed. They were flailing away, taking up space in the middle of the walkway. Dad stepped in front of us, his broad frame acting as a shield as these two men went at each other like dogs.

'Hey boys, settle down,' Dad said. I was shocked to hear him call them boys. 'There are families trying to go through here.'

Holding a blanket under one arm, Dad reached with his free arm to break it up. The men started laughing maniacally. Dad looked baffled, then annoyed. The men had been playfighting.

'Fuck off,' one of them said, with surprising venom. He thrust his chest and chin at Dad. His friend copied the pose. They shaped up.

'You wanna go?'

Their question was genuine. It left a gaping silence for my father to fill. I felt paralysed. Steve edged forward, as if he were thinking about helping out. But he was only fourteen. Dad was alone. The decision was his. *Did* he wanna go? The crowd pressed in around us. Dad's frame seemed to widen and grow taller. He shifted his stance to the balls of his feet, looming at the challengers. They took a step back, almost falling over each other, but they kept their fists raised.

'Mick,' Mum said.

Her voice made Dad glance back at us; at his cherished family. He exhaled, his shoulders dropping.

'C'mon kids,' he said, turning and shepherding us along. 'Let's go.'

I was relieved. Seeing Dad fight was unthinkable. But I also felt sorry for him. Wasn't it his right to cut loose and vent his fury? Did Mum just deny him the chance to clean up these two fools? Maybe she should've let him have his moment?

Dad was still holding the blanket.

'That's it, old man,' one of the drunks called after him. 'Walk away.'

'Yeah, walk away old man,' the other said.

I'd never heard Dad called old. Sure, he had grey hair. But he was a mountain of a man. He hadn't aged a day in my life.

On the long drive home, Dad was silent.

In our bunks that night, Steve said the two men didn't know how lucky they were that Dad had walked away. I'd been worrying for Dad, but Steve saw it differently.

'Dad could've killed 'em if he wanted to,' Steve said.

Now, as Adam and I shuffled away, I knew what it was to be my father. Only in my case, I was panicking and the danger hadn't passed. My attackers were coming after us. My head throbbed from the punch, but already I could feel pangs of shame. I'd been hit, in public. Now I was trying to get away. Around us, life seemed normal. There were shoppers walking by, a few cars passing, drivers peering at us.

'Just fuck off,' Adam said to our pursuers. 'Leave him alone.'

We reached a petrol station on the highway, the gang still close behind us.

I approached a driver filling up his car with petrol.

'Can you take us to the police station?' I said. 'Those blokes are after us.'

The driver, a young, clean-cut sort of guy, was surprisingly sympathetic, as if he'd seen this type of thing before. He told us to wait by the car. 'I'll just go in and pay,' he said. 'Then we'll go.'

Riz and his mates paced the footpath nearby. Riz gave the impression he was savage – eager to strike again – although I noted his reluctance to come any closer. Was he trying to impress his mates? I was vulnerable standing right there. Then Riz started coming at me. His friends stayed on the footpath, chanting.

'Get 'im, get 'im, fuck 'im up.'

The sight of Riz heading for me on his own gave me clarity. It eliminated the myth of numbers that I'd been sweating on since we first saw these boys back in Quayside. Five versus two – badly outnumbered. But now even Tremaine was standing back. The numbers game was simple: one on one. I felt a flush of defiance.

As soon as Riz was close enough I grabbed him and he grabbed me. As we grappled, my fear fell away. The action of fighting was not as bad as the anticipation. Riz wilted in my embrace. It was clear to both of us that I was stronger than he was. I lifted him off his feet and slammed his back against the car next to us. 'Hey watch the fuckin' car, man,' Riz said. His concern for someone else's property was convenient to his need to free himself. His voice had lost its menace. I was relieved. My aggression was controllable. I didn't go wild. My purpose was to quell the threat of being hit again. My arm went behind his neck and I twisted his head down his body. Then I shoved him again into the car, making sure I stayed close enough so he couldn't lash out. He was almost submissive.

'Keep the fuck back,' Adam said, warding off Riz's friends.

The kindly driver had returned. 'Stop it,' he said

'Told ya,' Riz whined. He'd lost his warrior's pose. He seemed more like a schoolboy trying to suck up to teacher. I let him go and he backed away.

The driver dropped us outside the police station. We didn't go in. The cops had enough to worry about.

I struggled with how I handled that attack. To run away was to violate the rules of manhood according to every 1980s action movie I ever memorised. Then again, I reckoned it was part of growing up. Dad once told me, 'No matter how tough you think you are, there's always someone tougher; someone willing to go further to win.'

I could tell Adam felt some pity for me. He'd seen through my shield of bravado. And he had his own regrets. He said he should have thrown some punches in my defence. But that never crossed my mind. I was bigger than he was. It was on me. I hoped he didn't lose sleep over it. I was just pleased he knew me well – that I was more bluster than buster. Hard as it was to concede, I was a boy of reason, my father's son.

35

A Poke in the Eye

After my dismal audition for the big league with St Kilda reserves, it felt good to have the big brown Stingray on my chest again – like coming home.

Two things had changed during my time away from the Under 18 competition: the grounds had softened up due to winter rain, and Hutchy had brought in new players to cover those missing from AFL reserves duties. (Sydney didn't want to send Smithy back to us; he'd kicked plenty of goals in his matches for the Swans and was often named among the best players.) The result was a stronger squad. It turned out our bottom-age players (sixteen-year-olds turning seventeen) were some of the best going round. The names roll off my tongue just remembering their footy exploits: Matthew Joy; Ryan Aitken; Matthew Hose; Stevie Meddings. Top-age players were inspired and lifted too – guys like Brad Lloyd, Brad Burns, Laurie Knott and Damon Lawrence. We played Geelong Falcons at Rye and beat them. Then we set ourselves to take down our nemesis Central at Frankston. Hutchy used 'Scratcha' Lielnors – the kid who'd helped me up the mountain in pre-season – as a tagger against top Dragon (and Brisbane Bears draftee) Aaron Lord. It was a winning move. Next, we took down Northern

Knights, the competition favourite. Smithy was back from Sydney for that one; he took ten marks and had thirty possessions. Watto broke a tag and kicked four goals. Whitey controlled the ruck and tapped the ball to winning crumbers.

But our biggest win, by one hundred and fifty-four points, came in a rematch with Murray Bushrangers. Whitey took thirteen marks. Smithy took fifteen marks and kicked ten goals.

We had now won eight out of our last nine games, losing only to the ladder leaders, Western Jets.

Hutchy was showing his experience and expertise in managing the side. He was a first-class coach – empathetic yet demanding, patient but not indulgent. One day in a game at Waverley Park, he pulled me aside before the huddle. It was three-quarter time. We were losing badly.

'What's the matter with you?' he said.

'Nothing. Why?'

'You've been walking a lot,' he said. 'Are you injured or just not interested?'

This was the first time he'd scolded me. I knew enough about him by now to understand it wasn't personal. I might have been one of his favourites but that didn't buy me leniency. I couldn't argue with this approach. As Dad would say, I had to wear it. Where once I would have been jogging or sprinting, I was now trudging. My fitness was slipping. I wasn't getting to enough contests. My binge drinking was robbing my body of a chance to recover physically, and my eating habits were sloppy, particularly on hangover Sundays. I was still training hard at the gym and football sessions, but I'd stopped pounding the streets. The light-as-a-kite feeling I had in summer and autumn was gone. I knew it was too late in the season to get it back. Fitness took time, and I'd wasted a lot of it. My legs felt like they belonged to a plodding veteran.

But I wasn't completely useless. I still did the basics well: a kick, a handball, a tackle. I protected my teammates. I beat my man most times in one-on-one tussles. I was still courageous. I just wasn't dashing. In short, I'd lost a yard or two in a game where a couple of yards make all the difference.

Hutchy's next move hit me where it hurt. In the huddle, with everyone listening, he poked an accusing finger at my chest. 'PK, if you don't go and get ten possessions in this last quarter you won't hold your spot in the side next week.'

Numbers game.

'Okay, Hutch,' I vowed. 'I will.'

I was no longer out to impress him. I was desperately avoiding his disappointment.

For the last quarter I was moved to a forward flank. Straight away I collided with one of the Eastern boys in the middle of the ground. Tempers flared. Briefly we tangled. Another boy hit me in the face, grabbing at my cheek and pressing my eyeball back into my skull. Pain shot through every nerve in my body.

'Cunt,' I said. My carnal reaction to this indignity was barbaric.

For the rest of the game I bolted from contest to contest, craving collisions that might assuage my revenge lust. Along the way, I was reunited with the feeling of compiling kicks and handballs. Meanwhile, others in the team were finding a similar flow. We went from trailing to leading to a rousing win. A smiling Hutchy met me on the ground after the final siren.

'Know how many you had that quarter?' he asked, clearly impressed with the number of possessions I'd gathered.

'Yeah, twelve.' I was surprised at the defiance in my voice.

'How'd you know?'

'I counted.'

'Should get someone to smack you in the face every week,' he said.

I couldn't help but smile with him.

'Well done mate,' he said.

Three words to soothe a fraying footballer's soul.

36

Who's Got the Petrol?

At school, I had an idea. I couldn't say where it came from exactly, but I knew it started with *The Wonder Years*. The show first aired when I was twelve, the same age as the main characters Kevin Arnold and his best friends Paul and Winnie. We were all starting high school. Though it was set in the late 1960s–early 70s, it felt like we were all growing up together. Kevin spoke about his anxieties, dreams and regrets through a narrator – an adult version of himself. There was a lot of Kevin in me. We were both working-middle class, with strong father figures. My mates used to say Dad *was* Jack Arnold. I took that as a compliment, although I knew my father was easier going. Another strong connection was place. The Arnold family lived in a housing estate that looked like mine, albeit with wider street and cars, and a Joe Cocker-led soundtrack of classic sixties music. In the first episode, the narrator said, 'There's no pretty way to put this: I grew up in the suburbs. I guess most people think of the suburbs as a place with all the disadvantages of the city, and none of the advantages of the country, and vice versa. But, in a way, those really were the wonder years for us there in the suburbs. It was a kind of golden age for kids.' He was talking about us, wasn't he?

Most of my friends felt the same way. After every episode on a Sunday night, we'd talk about it at school on Monday.

It was Doc who broke the news to us in mid-1993 – after six years, the show had been axed.

'The last episode's coming up,' he announced. 'A one-hour finale.'

I felt numb at the thought. I watched the last episode alone, in tears. We were breaking up after so many lovely years. In the final scene, the narrator told us what ended up happening to the Arnolds. When he said Kevin's father died of a heart attack two years later, I bawled my eyes out. The show finished with the words: 'I remember a place, a town, a house, like a lot of other houses, with a yard like a lot of other yards, on a street like a lot of other streets. And the thing is, after all these years, I still look back with wonder.'

Losing Kevin Arnold was like losing a mate. I dwelled on scenes I loved the most. One got me thinking about my idea.

When Kevin's friend Paul gave a junior-high valedictory speech at the end of the fourth series, I liked his address so much I wrote it down in my diary, word for word: 'The future rushes at us and we, in turn, stand ready, armed with our hopes, our dreams and our memories.'

It hit me that our final year was flying by. We shouldn't let the occasion pass without doing something memorable. But what? I rang Adam with a vision – I told him we should do something to leave our mark on the school. His enthusiasm surprised and thrilled me. We started talking about matches and petrol.

With Doc agreeing to join us, we rode to the school late one freezing, moonless night in the middle of the week. I steered one-handed through the back gate, carrying a rusted jerry can of diesel from my father's garage. It was darker than dark. No stars in the sky. We were wearing tracksuits, hoodies and beanies. I felt like a criminal mastermind leading a heist. None of us mentioned the ongoing Arson Squad investigation into the million-dollar fire in the science wing that had made front-page headlines only months earlier. We were too caught up in the moment.

'Can't believe we're doing this,' Doc said. 'This is gnarly.'

'Let's do it quickly and bail,' I said.

Looking for a space on the field where the grass was longest, Adam pointed to the nearest portable classroom.

'That was where we locked Mr Ball in,' Adam said. 'Remember?'

Mr Ball was a sensitive young teacher who we'd teased mercilessly for months on end in middle school. One day we all rushed out after his class and used a padlock to keep him inside until he broke down begging.

'We made him cry,' said Adam, who was now taking a leak. The grass in front of him was steaming. 'What pricks we were. Don't step in that.'

'Whose idea was it to lock him in?' I said.

'Probably yours.'

I hoped he was wrong, although I couldn't argue. It was no longer funny to reminisce about how cruel we'd been to some teachers.

Doc was scoping the grass nearby. 'I reckon we can do it here. Who's got the petrol?'

'I'll pour it,' I said.

We did a fine job. Not a drop out of place. Then Adam lit the grass. The flames spelled out the smouldering words: CLASS OF 1993.

It was very American. Dad would have been disappointed we were copying the yanks. But nobody could fault our handiwork.

We stood and watched, as fishermen might look up at an unusually large boat passing slowly along a narrow river.

'I thought it'd be more exciting,' Adam said.

'Smells nice,' I said.

Within a few minutes, the fire was out. We rode our bikes home, giggling. Next day, I made sure I was early. The grass we had torched was perfectly brown. You had to stand on your toes for the best view but there it was. CLASS OF 1993. Some kids wandered by, making their way to the sand dunes up the back of the oval for their morning fags. An hour went by, then morning recess. No one seemed to notice our inscription on the oval. Some students walked right over it without looking down. There were no announcements over the loudspeaker. Not a hint of ruckus. At lunchtime, I sat with Adam and a few other boys, gazing at the dead patch and complaining.

'That's the problem with the place,' I said. 'No one gives a shit. We'll have to do something bigger.'

37

Natalie

It was the last Friday in July, one of those damp afternoons that made you dislike winter for dragging on. Police were out in force, as they had been for weeks. Along with an influx of officers from patrolling departments (mounted, dogs squad etc.), more than fifty detectives were now on the Frankston killer case. The door-knocking went on to no avail. Pressure was building on the Homicide Squad to make an arrest.

With Victoria Police putting 'one hundred and fifty per cent effort' into solving the case, it was difficult to see how the killer could remain free much longer. A $50,000 bounty was put up. Detectives told us via press conferences they were confident of making an arrest in the 'very near future'. An eight-man taskforce was working on the case 'around the clock'.

Plenty of tip-offs were coming in, but so many led nowhere. Among the calls one afternoon was a report from a postwoman delivering letters along Skye Road, near John Paul College. She said there was a man wearing a blue cap sitting in a parked car with no number plates. The postie told the cops that the car was near the entrance to a track between two golf courses: Peninsula and Long Island. The path was a thoroughfare used by teenagers from the nearby Catholic school.

Two young constables from Frankston Police were dispatched to Skye Road, where they found the car empty. The officers scribbled down the make and model – a 1974 yellow Toyota Corona – and noted the registration sticker on the windscreen. It looked to them like a stolen car.

At about two-thirty, shortly after the police returned to the station, a seventeen-year-old girl from John Paul College crossed Skye Road on her way home. Her name was Natalie Russell. School hadn't finished but Natalie's final class for the day was a free. She usually rode her bike to and from school but with the sky looking threatening that morning, her mother had given her a lift.

Two boys from John Paul College saw Natalie walking home towards the path between the golf courses. One of them was my friend Juan.

'Seeya Nat,' Juan said, before heading north along Skye Road to his dad's house.

Natalie waved and kept going. It was no more than a ten-minute walk through to the other end of the trail.

An hour later, the rest of the school's students headed home, many on foot or bikes along the same track that Natalie had taken. No one saw anything unusual. Darkness and rain were falling. Natalie hadn't made it home. Her parents rang police and reported their daughter missing.

For the rest of us, it was just another Friday night. I was at home getting grumpy, watching Collingwood get thrashed by Essendon at the MCG. My mate Juan, a fanatical Bombers supporter, had caught the train to the game after farewelling Natalie. At the match that night he claimed to have marked the ball in the grandstand. 'It was a Timmy Watson kick.'

By the time I went to bed there was a helicopter over the Skye Road track, cops on horseback, and State Emergency Service volunteers – all out looking for Natalie. Two of the SES searchers walked slowly with their torches. One of them shone his light on what looked like a hole in a wire fence. They held their breath, pointed. One of the holes was big enough for a man to walk through. A big man.

38

Whitey's Tears

Knowing nothing about the awful events of the night before, I arrived at Moorabbin on Saturday morning to play for the Stingrays in a mood close to elation. Mum and Dad had driven me to the game but we'd missed the news on the radio. The sun was warm enough on my neck not to wear a jacket as I strode in my black slacks and office shoes across the oval to the centre square, where my teammates were gathered. This ritual of pre-game greetings and banter had become comforting, one my favourite things to do. This was the only place I wanted to be, acting as one of Hutchy's trusted charges. I felt the same excitement as I did in round one, although the season was nearing its conclusion, with finals approaching. Playing a game on the MCG was now a distinct possibility. Also, it was almost August. My eighteenth birthday was only weeks away.

I saw straight away something was wrong. Our ruckman Jeff White was standing all alone. He was crying. This tall, slender boy who'd built a reputation as an AFL prospect and grinned his way through a marvellous season, his bright face beaming every time you looked his way, was so upset he didn't even bother trying to catch his tears.

'What's up, mate?' Whitey's painful expression gave me shivers. 'You okay?'

My smile felt stupid so I dropped it.

'He killed another one,' Whitey said. 'She was from our school.'

There was a windless silence. Some of the other boys nodded.

'It's fucked,' someone said.

'Who was she?' I asked. I knew a few girls from John Paul College because I'd been to quite a few parties with Juan and Leo.

'Nat Russell,' Whitey said. 'She was in Year 12. She didn't come home from school.'

'Shit, that's awful mate. Sorry.'

I wanted to picture Natalie. I thought that might help me comfort Whitey. I wished I could give him a hug.

'Inside boys,' Crouchy called out. In that moment it seemed wrong that the game was going ahead; that the world just carried on. Whitey sniffed, picked up his bag, and headed for the change room.

Our opponent was Bendigo. We won by one hundred and six points. Records show the score was 20.24.144 to 5.8.38. Shayne Smith wasn't there. He was playing his last game for Sydney Swans reserves after filling in no fewer than seven times. Rumour had it he was turning out better performances than the established men in the squad. With the national draft nearing, and the legendary Ron Barassi coaching Sydney's senior side, Smithy was on the brink of the big time.

I played a decent game on that mournful day at Moorabbin, picking up twenty-four touches and kicking two goals. The newspaper report had me in the best players for the first time since

June. Young forward Matthew Joy kicked four goals. He'd been improving every week since representing Victoria at the Under 17 National Championships. Another happy-go-lucky player, he could do everything well, and seemed adaptable in varying conditions – a coach's dream. BA was back in the side after his AFL reserves stint and hadn't lost any fitness or self-confidence. One newspaper article noted that the Southern Stingrays 'smalls' were 'once again very well fed by the improving Jeff White'. Despite his grief, Whitey kicked two goals and had sixteen possessions, including six marks. Everyone at the game noted his grit. Suggestions about him being AFL-material were no longer mere murmurings.

We sang our theme song after the win but the celebrations ended there. The news of Natalie Russell's murder had filtered through to parents and others at the game. She had been found at about eleven o'clock the night before. The SES volunteers who'd discovered the hole in the fence had trained their torches on the ground beyond the wire. Natalie's body was there. Crime scene investigators hurried to do their work. They noted the ground had been churned up. The teenager had fought for her life, against an attacker with a knife. The poor Russell parents, Carmel and Brian, were informed early the next day, and another family member held a press conference mid-afternoon, about the time we were finishing our game.

The only positive news was that a pathologist had found a piece of skin at the crime scene. It didn't belong to Natalie. Also, a thirteen-year-old boy who'd been walking along the track the previous afternoon reported seeing a large man walk past with his hands in his pockets. Lead detectives were only just hearing about the suspicious yellow car that had been parked on Skye Road. The car was gone, but its registration sticker now gave investigators the name and address of its owner.

39

Taxi to Nowhere

I went out to the Frankston pubs that night and wished I hadn't. I wasn't consciously drinking away the Natalie Russell tragedy, but I certainly wrote myself off faster and harder than usual. Deep down, I knew that if I got drunk, I didn't have to care so much about anything. It felt good to not care.

Mum always told me not to hate anyone. But I knew I hated the murderer. And I think she allowed me this one. Not that I thought he was evil, as everyone seemed to be saying. To call him evil suggested he wasn't human. It gave him an excuse. There was no excuse for what this pathetic shadow-dwelling man was doing. No reason.

After slamming down my drinks at The Grand, I went roaming. At the 21st Century Dance Club I went round and round on the dance floor in a daze, before ducking into The Pelly Bar to throw down a few more bourbons. In this mood, I wasn't socialising. I was slapping backs and flopping my arms around some people I knew, then lurching on my way. My pretence was that I was everyone's friend. The truth was I was withdrawing from others.

Now, I was drinking to lose control of my senses. I no longer spent time in the sweet spot of tipsiness, with all its confidence and fun and flirtations. I took great mouthfuls of beer and bourbon to get to the other side of the drunken curve, where time evaporated and left me conscious of only one thing. I was sad and lonely and worried about my future. The year would soon be finished, and I was struggling at school and relationships. Outside my family and mates, I didn't feel like anyone could love me. No girls wanted me in the way I wanted them. To whisper softly and be gentle and playful. I'd always been confident I could find a clear path through any doubts. My mother told me when I was little boy, I was going to be great. Until this year, I never doubted her.

I swayed my way through the sparce crowds in the pubs, my drunkenness granting me permission to move to the music without dancing. I constantly wandered, stopping only for toilet breaks and to lean on the bar and order another one.

I passed out some time after midnight.

Next thing I knew I was in a taxi with an older friend from the local footy club. I was in the back seat, my head resting against the cold glass of the window. It must have been two or three o'clock in the morning.

The driver was talking to us. He seemed agitated.

'Where do you want me to pull up?' he said.

I was familiar with some of the drivers who worked Saturday nights for Frankston Taxis. A couple of them were dads from my estate. I didn't know this cabbie and he didn't know or trust us. We were approaching a dead end.

'Where, exactly?' The driver was saying. 'Are you boys sure you live here?'

It took me a few seconds to realise we were in another suburb, north of Seaford, about five kilometres from my home. How did I get here? I couldn't remember anything of the last few hours.

'You're not gunna do a runner, are yas?' the driver said.

'Nah,' said my mate, winking at me.

'Don't do it fellas,' the driver said. His eyes found me in the rear-vision mirror. He'd taken one hand off the steering wheel and was searching for something under his seat. I heard a rattling noise, metal against plastic. The cabbie was brandishing a Club Lock, like the one Steve used to lock up his steering wheel. 'I better see some money before I stop,' he said.

'I've got some dosh,' I said, my voice a rough croak. 'If I've still got me wallet.'

Fumbling in my jeans pocket, I was relieved to find my wallet, in all its Coca-Cola-branded Velcro glory. It was full of shrapnel — loose change from rounds I didn't remember ordering.

My friend directed the cabbie to stop at the end of the cul-de-sac. The fare was only about eight bucks.

I was still digging for coins in my wallet. 'Might have enough here.'

The driver looked relieved. 'I've had a few runners in the last month,' he told us. 'I've got to take precautions.' He placed his right hand back on the wheel to show us he wasn't planning to use his weapon.

That was when I heard my mate's door fly open. He took off quick as a punch, sprinting into the silent night. Without thinking, I copied.

I'd only ever done a runner once before. It was about a year earlier. Adam and I had been hanging out at a derelict house with some of our dope-smoking friends. About six of us crammed into a cab to get back to Seaford. Someone started singing the Kris Kross song 'Jump'. Others joined in. Adam and I looked at each other with trepidation. Then they ran for it, with Adam and me following, into some scrubland. There was laughter as we scattered, but it wasn't fun. I would never forget the look of disappointment on the driver's face when he realised what was going on. I pictured Dad, who used to drive taxis back in Seymour. He would have been devastated to know I'd run out on a man working crap nightshifts to provide for his family.

Now I'd done it again.

Blundering into an unfamiliar, dimly lit street, I tried to find my mate. But he was gone. The freezing air shocked me awake. I was panting. Heavy footsteps pounded after me. The cabbie, defying everything I knew of the taxi-driver code of staying with your car, was close behind.

'I'll fuckin' kill you,' he shouted.

I scampered like a sewer rat through a gap in a fence and out onto an empty road. The driver's outburst faded into silence, but for all I knew he was still coming for me. My legs ached and I wished I could collapse in the gutter. I scaled a wooden fence into an overgrown backyard. Gasping for breath, I went to ground, curled up among some tall weeds. A dog barked and I hoped like hell I was on the right side of the fence. I wasn't. A muscular mongrel came tearing out of the dark, pulling up just short of my face. The snarling mutt edged closer, more than ready to bark or bite. An outdoor light flicked on, illuminating the yard and my hiding place. I wasn't among weeds. I'd landed in a small marijuana plantation. I swore under my breath. The dog snapped at me in vain, and I bounded back over the fence like an Olympic high jumper. In the mad scramble I thought I heard someone rush out of the house, but I couldn't be certain.

Sore and sorry, I sloped back the way I came. I'd sobered up enough to feel remorse coming on. I felt bad for the taxi driver. I wanted to give him the fare we owed him. But back at the cul-de-sac, the taxi was nowhere to be seen. My Coca-Cola wallet was gone too. I faintly recalled it slipping from my pocket back in the dope patch. I was cursing myself when a growling voice made me startle. I heard him before I saw him.

'Got ya,' said the taxi driver, so close I could feel the heat in his words. He lunged at me as I took off up the street. A rush of air brushed my ear as the cabbie's Club Lock flew past my head and clanged onto the bitumen.

'Argh,' the driver said. 'Fuck it.'

It wasn't over. I'd glimpsed the taxi parked further up the street and now heard its engine roar. I veered off into a front yard, huddling behind some flowers. As the taxi drew near I saw the yard didn't have a fence. No protection. The cab slowed to a crawl, its blinding sidelight creeping from house to house, searching for me. It was time to give up; to take my beating. What a debacle. Crouched among the flowers with the harsh spotlight about to hit me, I wondered if any of my mates would have been up to anything this stupid. I couldn't imagine any of my teammates or school friends getting themselves into a spot like this. This didn't feel normal.

A moment before the light hit me, as I was about to stand and surrender, the cabbie killed the switch. Darkness enfolded me. He'd given up.

'You prick,' he yelled into the night. Tyres spun hard, and he drove away.

I stayed hunched in the garden for a few more minutes, not daring to push my luck too soon. When I finally headed for home I took the back streets, wanting to avoid traffic, especially police cars. Rolling my ankle on a gutter beside Kananook Creek, I staggered on the steep bank and ended up knee-deep in the freezing, stinking water. The sky was turning from black to grey. It was morning. And I smelled like shit. People would soon be up and about. I hobbled onto Emanuel Drive, my jeans dripping black sludge.

When Mum woke me near midday, she took one look at me and said, 'What have you done?' I told her the whole story, including how I lost my wallet in someone's backyard.

'Get your shoes on,' she said. 'You're going around there to ask for it back.'

On the drive there, Mum was stony silent, asking only for directions. When we pulled up out the front of the house, she motioned for me to go in. I was on my own. I knocked on the door and waited. The owner eventually opened it. He was holding my wallet.

'PK,' he said, 'I was wondering when you might show up.'

Turned out he was an old friend of a friend. I remembered him as a jokey kind of bloke. But now his face revealed none of its pleasantness.

'Sorry mate,' I said.

He nodded gravely and patted his dog, who'd sidled up beside him. 'At first I thought you were after me plants. Didn't know you were the type.'

'I'm not.'

'I know,' he said. He'd spoken to my mate, who'd jumped the cab with me. They knew each other.

234

'So you got your mum to drive you round?' He smirked, looking over my shoulder at our car, before fixing me with a hard stare and tossing my wallet at me. 'Be more careful next time.'

'Thanks,' I said. I walked away, a coward humiliated.

That night, as I was writing in my diary, Dad came into my room. He wasn't scornful or mad. His eyes were wells of disappointment. And that was so much worse. Tears edged their way down my cheeks. I let them fall.

'Mum told me what happened,' he said. My shoulders started to go. He didn't touch me or comfort me in any way. 'Can I make an observation?'

I wiped my eyes and nodded.

'I see you go to the gym every day. You're pretty good at that, working hard to improve your body. Maybe it's time you did some something to improve your personality and attitude.'

Dad's words condemned me. When he left my room I wanted the ceiling to fall in and the walls to collapse in on me. It would have been a relief. Eventually I slept. When I woke, it was to the sound of the news on the telly in the loungeroom. The cops had arrested a suspect in the murders of Elizabeth Stevens, Debbie Fream and Natalie Russell.

'Got 'im,' Mum said. 'Beauty.'

40

At Last

———————

That Monday at school it was as if spring had come early. The salt air felt lighter, easier to breathe. The droning police helicopters had finally left our skies. The newspapers, radio bulletins and television news broadcasts celebrated the killer's capture but soon they too would move on.

Natalie Russell's death changed the lives of many of my friends. A funeral was held at John Paul College. It was the biggest anyone could remember, reminding me of Mrs Mac's comment: 'If you want a lot of people at your funeral, you'd better die young.'

A photograph from the family of Natalie showed her warm, pretty eyes; her long, dark hair resting on her shoulders. It was a school picture. You could just see the collar of her uniform. I thought she looked cheeky. She hadn't quite broken into a full smile but you expected she might have after the flash. Was a friend standing off to one side of the lens, trying to make her laugh?

Natalie's last brave act was to help police catch the killer. The scrap of skin she had torn from her attacker, which was found at the scene, would become a vital piece of DNA evidence.

Using the registration details from the yellow Toyota Corona on Skye Road, the Homicide Squad honed in on a twenty-one-year-old suspect. He lived within the triangle drawn up by Inspector Claude Minisini. He also had cuts on his hands. One wound – almost three centimetres long – held the attention of detectives.

Hours later, the killer confessed to killing Natalie, Elizabeth and Debbie. 'I did the three of 'em,' he said. On that stormy night back in June, he'd watched Elizabeth Stevens get off the bus. He forced her to hold his hand, as if they were a couple. At Lloyd Park reserve, he choked and stabbed her to death. He confirmed he had assaulted the woman outside the soccer club, near Seaford railway station, then caught a train to Kananook and waited in Debbie Fream's car. The ambush on Natalie Russell had been planned; he cut holes in the fence with pliers earlier in the day. He said he didn't care who the victim was, as long as it was a girl or woman. Asked why, the killer said: 'Just hate 'em.'

He was charged with three counts of murder and one of abduction. A trial was set for December.

41

Almost Spiritual

A week or so after the killer was captured, Mrs Mac announced to the twelve eager members of her inaugural Year 12 English Literature class that she was taking us on a mid-week, late-night excursion to an amateur Shakespeare play – the comedy *Much Ado About Nothing*.

The play itself was like watching a foreign film without subtitles. The jokes went way over my head. I laughed along to pretend I was getting it. While I had started reading more books, my comprehension of literature was an ongoing frustration. And understanding Shakespeare on stage was another literary challenge I was sure to fail. The experience, however, meant more to me than the dialogue, or even the story.

Sitting there in the dark, with all eyes on the stage, I was able to give in to a surprising exhilaration. I took pleasure in the rhythm of sounds and the power of voices. I was in awe of the actors' confidence and energy. As the play went on, I let my mind wander outside my usual pattern of thoughts. I daydreamed about places I'd never been. I imagined myself as the globe-trotting star of the play I was watching – a handsome master of speech, changing the mood of the room with a shrug or wink. I found myself getting envious of the actors' world. What a strange delight it was to discover I could love something different to everything I'd known. It was like finding a spectacular headland on a coast I thought was straight and plain.

There was only one other time in my life I could compare the experience to. It was during a school camp the year before, to a place called Rubicon, a former timber town in the Yarra Ranges National Park. Our Outdoor Education leader was a bear of a man named Ron Jungalwalla. He had a brown beard, full cheeks and kind, dark eyes. Back in Frankston his size would have made him a menacing figure but he had a gentleness about him, in a gregarious way. His passion was nature. I admired Ron immediately and followed him like a tail-wagging puppy on one of our treks along a trail shaded by ancient trees. We were off to camp in the bush overnight. The forest smelled of eucalyptus, ferns and wet bark. Everything was new to me, but I had a strange feeling I'd been here before.

'Just wait till you see where I'm taking you,' Ron told us. 'It's heaven on earth.'

With Ron now leading our hike, we were feeling much more at one with nature. But when we eventually stopped walking, after hours of anticipation, Ron's mood soured.

'Oh, no,' Ron said. 'No, no, no.'

We were looking down a path at an ugly mud clearing. Ron's idyllic camping spot had been ruined. It reminded me of our old housing estate from back in my toddlerhood; the ground criss-crossed with tyre marks.

Ron threw back his head and stomped his feet. 'Why do they have to do it here!?' He seemed more bear-like than ever. Then he became rigid. I could tell he was trying to compose himself. He led us into the muddy clearing. A tear was running into his whiskers. His chest was heaving.

'See these tracks? Bloody dirt bikes,' he said. 'They've torn the place apart. They come here and ride around until there's nothing left to destroy.'

I imagined there must have been a dozen bikes to leave so many scars in the soft earth.

'I want you to remember this,' Ron said. 'This is environmental vandalism. Never forget it.'

He looked so sad as to be grieving. It shocked me to see, for the first time, a big man cry. I knew it was good for me to witness. I too was becoming emotional, as were the other children.

I nodded and made my pledge.

All of this was a shock to my senses but the revelation was still to come. We pitched our tents and slept on the mud. I woke up in the middle of the night. The mountain river, called Royston, was loud as a passing train. I unzipped the front flap and went to look at the rushing water shining in the moonlight. Ron was sitting there. I didn't know what to say so I just nodded. He seemed content again. 'It's a beautiful place isn't it?' he said.

Together we gazed at the stars. The sky was so bright with them I could barely see any black.

'Shit, that's unreal, is it always like that?'

Ron laughed.

'I think I need to get out more,' I said.

Ron told me I'd done well on the camp. He sounded surprised. I wondered whether our teachers might have told him I could be a handful. Then he said goodnight and left me alone. I sat and studied the stars. I felt the energy and promise in the sky. It was a spiritual moment, I suppose. The universe was too big to explore but I felt an urgency to get started.

How this sensation was replicated by sitting in a small theatre I couldn't say, but it was startling. I let the moment take hold of me. When the lights came up I felt changed; improved, even.

Mrs Mac gave some of us a lift home. I was the last one to be dropped off. I was still buzzing from the night out, trying to hang onto the experience by replaying it in my head. When I got out of the car all I said was, 'Cheers, seeya.' I want to go back to that moment and say what I really felt; that I was so grateful to Mrs Mac for showing me parts of life I didn't know about. I want to say that she was amazing for taking an interest in me, the real me; and that thanks to her, I wanted to be better than I was.

When Mrs Mac drove away I stood on the nature strip in the faint light of the pole across the road, the one I used to kick a ball at. I didn't want to go inside straight away. I breathed the quiet night air. Everyone was asleep. This was my home. But for how much longer?

42

Milestone

I turned eighteen in August. But I didn't feel like celebrating.

First, I was injured and couldn't play football for two weeks. I got hurt while filling in for the Seaford Under 18s team one Sunday morning during a week off Stingrays duties.

I'd always thought of myself as pretty much damage-proof, but this injury was different to all the others. It was a groin strain. I'd slipped while diving for a mark in the dirt covering the cricket pitch at the Seaford ground. The pain started beside my testicles and shot up through my stomach. I pleaded with Hutchy to let me play but he told me to rest for two weeks. I put the injury down to bad luck but I'd been stupid to play another game on top of my other commitments, not to mention all those late nights out. My body and mind were showing signs of wear and tear.

Soon after, I passed my driving test. My lessons with Dad had prepared my impeccably. I no longer had to sneak into my brother's car and go joyriding at night. I could drive anywhere, any time. I could pull stumps and drive around Australia if I wanted. If only I had a car. Still, the licence alone told me I'd shifted another gear. I wasn't a kid anymore.

While I rested and regained my strength, I savoured the hint of winter's end. I could feel the air getting warmer. The cold months couldn't hold on much longer. The transition to spring was the loveliest of all seasonal changes. Gnats danced in the sunshine. Lawns went wild, you could smell them, and the sound of lawn mowers became normal and reassuring. Bare branches on the aisle of giant trees outside the railway station sprouted puffs of red-green foliage. Bees buzzed in the gardens, sounding as happy as the people. 'How about this weather?' The swamp bred new armies of supersized mozzies that came after you at dusk. Nesting magpies started swooping kids on bikes.

September brought with it high winds and clear blue skies. Neighbours emerged like bears from hibernation, blinking in the light. On the foreshore, white flowers covered the tea tree like blankets of fallen snow. It was a sign from nature that the snapper were in season and football finals were just around the corner – for those athletes whose groins weren't too painful.

At school, teachers started asking us Year 12 students about our plans for the future. I still didn't have any answers. Mrs Mac again suggested journalism to me. But I suspected my grades wouldn't be good enough to get into a university course.

'You could go for a cadetship,' she said.

'Maybe,' I said. I didn't want to say I didn't know what a cadetship was. I'd only ever heard about trade apprenticeships.

43

The Big Stage

We had made it. I had made it. It was early September, and the Stingrays were playing an elimination final against Geelong Falcons. At the MCG. Our match was a curtain raiser to the first AFL final under lights. In a few hours, Essendon would play Carlton in front of ninety thousand people.

We entered the vast, white-walled change rooms under the newly named Great Southern Stand with eyes wide, as if we'd discovered Superman's Fortress of Solitude.

Our captain Ben Delarue spoke for all of us. 'How good is this?'

I had a ball with me. I bounced it on the floor and it rebounded into my twitching hands. Other players did the same. The echoing wallop of leather on concrete filled the nervous silence. My stomach started churning.

Benny was clapping his hands. 'Here we go, boys.'

Our star forward Shayne Smith smiled at the sight of us, with not a hint of tension in his broad, handsome face. Jeff White was laughing, Brett Anthony nodding his head. Dean Watson's expression was unreadable, as usual. Watto's lips were pursed. Four days earlier he was awarded the Morrish Medal for being the league's best and fairest.

I took a moment to silently congratulate myself for making it this far. This was the dream I'd had since I was old enough to worship heroes. I was tired of not knowing what it looked and felt like.

Hutchy's pre-game speech was clear. Clean hands. Support each other. Do the little things well. Be bold. Show us your courage. His manner was always warm. No one made a sound as he was getting into his address. When his voice rose to emphasise a point, my skin flickered with excitement.

I was less impressed when Hutchy came to me for 'a quick word'. His tone worried me.

'I'm gunna start you on the bench,' he said. My heart stopped. I hadn't been near the bench all season. 'I'm just not sure you can run out the game and I wanna use you in a slightly different way.'

He pressed a hand onto my shoulder, holding eye contact. The gesture was meant to console me. It wasn't an apology.

'We still need you running and attacking when you get out there,' he said. 'Get fired up when you come on.'

'I understand,' I said.

Hutchy had been more than patient in waiting for me to recapture my early season form. I was as strong as ever across the chest and shoulders, but my legs had lost their zip; my ability to feel like I was flying. The groin injury didn't help. During my two-week injury lay-off the team had lost a game to the Western Jets and beaten Eastern Ranges. I came back into the side for our last home and away game, a must-win match against the Falcons at Kardinia Park in Geelong. The groin still wasn't right, although I told Hutchy I'd recovered. I'd kept moving throughout the game, but I could only jog. When I kicked the ball, a dull pain shot up into my gut. We had won the game, with little help from me.

Now, with only minutes to go before our big MCG clash, all I could think about was how long I'd be spending on the sidelines.

Then Hutchy motioned me over again. Apparently one of us was missing. Another backman was running late. 'You're starting down back, not on the pine,' Hutchy said. 'Don't let me down mate. Stretch that groin.'

Beauty.

Just before we ran out, Smithy moved among us, quietly revving us up. 'Let's go, mate, today's the day, doesn't get better than this.' Though he wasn't our skipper, he looked ready to carry the lot of us on his shoulders. He wanted to show everyone he was the best teenage footballer in the country.

'Go get 'em boys,' yelled Hutchy.

We bit down on our mouthguards and roared like lions on wild plains. Together, the Southern Stingrays of 1993 charged up the players' race, leading us to the world's most magnificent sporting field. The path was uphill, steep enough to demand a heavy breath. Stepping out into the natural light, we saw the grandstands first – tall as mountains, sheer as cliffs.

The MCG opened its arms as we ran onto our field of dreams. We were welcomed by a warm spring day; not even a breeze inside the great colosseum. The turf smelled like the backyard five minutes after Dad had cut it.

The match lingers in my mind as a series of haphazard flashbacks. My movements were timid, inspired by hesitance and fear. I didn't want my groin to rip, so I avoided collisions and sharp turns. At the start of the season, I performed – I lived! – for Hutchy and the team. Now, I was self-serving; a shadow of a player. It was a structured game and we were winning from the start, so it was easy to read the play and collect handballs and short kicks. At half time I'd had about a dozen possessions. Statistically, it was a decent contribution to the collective effort. But I knew better, and so did the coach. Hutchy benched me for the start of the third quarter. I thought it was a reasonable move.

'We won't leave you there long,' he said. 'Stay warm.'

I didn't panic. It looked like we were going to win, mostly because Smithy was best on ground by a mile, taking mark after mark. He'd kicked a bagful of goals and he wasn't finished. The Falcons couldn't stop him. He'd had three opponents already. With our big weapon firing, we were right on course for a Grand Final. And I'd be well rested, ready to give more of myself.

I watched from the bench as we dominated the game in the third quarter. BA, Watto and Shane Quinn were sharing the ball with superior energy and skill. With the crowd building in the grandstands, there were now tens of thousands of people watching us. They witnessed Jeff White jumping in the ruck against an impressive teenager called Matthew Primus. Whitey was younger and more athletic than any of the other ruckmen. At the same time, Adam White, our long-limbed backman, was showing just how much he'd grown in stature over winter. This game was his best yet.

Hutchy phoned the bench and told me to go to the forward line. I bolted as quickly as I dared to the outer wing, where I finally did something memorable. Benny kicked the ball to me from the backline. It was a similar set-up to the one I'd experienced at Waverley in my first game for St Kilda, when I dropped the Sherrin and made a fool of myself. This time, I didn't let it slip, despite one of the Falcons lunging to spoil me. He clamped onto me so I didn't play on. In the centre square, Watto was heading for our forward line, screaming for the ball.

'PK, PK, PK!'

My opponent was so close I could feel him panting on my neck. I should have handballed. It was the team thing to do. But my desire to have a second of glory, just one personal second, was overpowering. I swung the ball beyond the line of my body, tempting my opponent with it. With the ball on my palm like a champagne glass on a silver tray, I dipped my shoulder for extra authenticity and faked a handball. That motion acted as a starter's gun for my opponent, who let go of me to chase Watto. But the ball was never going that way. When I knew my opponent had bought the ruse, I spun away, shoulders-first, to the wing in front of a now crowded Great Southern Stand. No coach ever teaches a player to spin blindly. It cannot be taught. I was plagiarising Dermot Brereton (the ex-Hawthorn champ was a Frankston boy too – played his junior years at the same club that turned out Smithy). I'd practised the move in my mind, before falling asleep on a thousand different nights back in Seaford. The crowd spurred me on as I turned around and straightened towards our distant goals. There was clapping and cheering. At least, that's how I remember it. My spirit was soaring. I was playing under lights at the MCG. I was gliding, not flailing. Look at me now!

The magic dust wore off all too soon. Too far out to score, I looked to kick to Smithy. I should have kicked with my reliable right boot, but a flash of groin pain made me drop the ball onto my left. The kick was a mongrel. It landed in no-man's land.

When the three-quarter time siren sounded, Hutchy gave his

final address for the day. After praising the team, he turned to me. 'PK, out on the wing, why didn't you kick it with your right?'

I gave no answer. We both knew.

'It looked like you were protecting your groin,' he said.

'Nah,' I said.

I would never forget his look of disappointment. I had betrayed Hutchy's trust. From the day we met, he'd only ever been honest with me. All he wanted in return was selflessness and effort. By lying to him about my injury, I had given him neither. That day at the MCG I was the worst thing a footballer could be – insignificant. Looking back, my soul aches in remembrance. Hutchy would have forgotten about it soon after – I was just one among hundreds of concerns he had that day – but I never would.

Though trailing, the Geelong Falcons were not about to give in and hand us the win. We were three or four goals in front of them. Our opponents had kicked straight for goal, which gave them a chance of an upset in the last quarter. Hutchy explained this to us but we didn't quite believe him. We had this. Smithy was on fire. He'd already bagged ten goals. Chad Liddell was the only other Stingray to have kicked more than one. He had two.

For the final quarter I was stationed in the forward line. The lights were all turned on by now. It was dusk. The stadium was almost packed. I was living my last childhood dream. I wasn't getting much of the ball, but I was getting to watch Smithy from close range. Having beaten all four opponents assigned to him, he was now contending with multiple Falcons backmen. Midway through the last quarter he kicked another goal. 'That's his twelfth!' someone shouted. Smithy had kicked two thirds of our eighteen goals.

With five minutes to go, the margin was reduced to fourteen points. The Falcons weren't conceding defeat, but we had time, and Smithy, on our side. When the ball was kicked to Smithy yet again I saw him take the best mark I'd ever seen. Three Falcons players were hanging onto him, like guards restraining a prisoner. Two of them were holding onto his left arm, one was reaching over his shoulder, trying to drag him away from the flight of the ball. Somehow Smithy still reached up to the sky with one hand, tapped the leather, almost caressed it, with his palm, waited for it to float past his chest, turned the same hand out and flattened it, catching the ball and shrugging his opponents off him one by one. There he stood, holding the ball, with the other teenagers sprawled around him.

The desperate Falcons replied with one goal, then another. Our lead was sliced to two points. Panic set in, but none of our stars in the centre square could seize the ball. Smithy prowled the forward line, ready to seal the game with his thirteenth goal. I stayed nearby, wishing I could do something, willing the siren to blow.

The Falcons somehow kicked another goal. They'd hit the front. Then another sailed through. Four in six minutes. We were ten points behind when the siren blasted. That was it. Our season was finished. We'd choked.

The silence in the change room said it all. Heads were down. I was staring at the wall. Hutchy couldn't talk. He was stunned, if not furious.

Smithy shattered the fragile air with frustration. 'Weak as fuckin' piss,' he said. His critique was directed at all of us. 'How did ya fuckin' lose that? We had 'em.'

No one dared answer.

Then Smithy said something utterly surprising.

'And you,' he said, pointing at one of our officials, 'you'd better not fuck up my chances of getting drafted again this year.'

The official looked dismayed.

It was the first time I'd heard our best player talk about his fear of falling short of the big league. He'd always appeared so self-confident. The rest of us thought he was a certainty to get picked up. Apparently, he still had doubts in himself, or at least the system.

Eventually, Hutchy got to his feet for one last speech. He thanked everyone – players, families, Crouchy, club volunteers – for their commitment. It had been a successful year, he said. Watto had won the Morrish Medal. Smithy had been named runner up in the VSFL *Herald-Sun* Coaches Award. (Later that month he would win our club best and fairest award; I led the vote count at the halfway mark of the season but barely polled a vote in the second half.) Seven of us had represented AFL reserves teams. Mick Prentice had been All-Australian Under 17s. Others had been selected in under-age Victorian teams.

As Hutchy was at pains to point out, there was more to football than winning and losing.

We showered and got changed into our slacks and polo shirts. I shook Hutchy's hand, gave him my thanks.

Above us, the Carlton versus Essendon game had started and the stadium was alive. Mum and Dad were in the grandstand waiting for me. They'd been to every one of my junior games since I was eight. They were always there.

I should have repaid them with my presence, at the very least, that night.

Instead, I told them I was going out on the town.

'Love ya mate,' Mum said. She could read my disappointment, maybe even embarrassment, about the game. She knew when her son hadn't played well, although she never said anything negative about my performances. 'Proud of you.'

'Well, look after yourself,' said Dad.

With my teammate Brad Burns, I went to a nightclub called The Metro, a hundred metres or so from the Victorian Parliament. I'd never been there before and I never went there again. We spent an hour inhaling tequila shots. Then I blacked out. I was woken the next morning in the Bourke Street gutter – literally in the gutter – by a street sweeper. The bright sun seemed to be laughing at me. Brad slouched over from his own resting place. He muttered something about grabbing breakfast.

'No,' I said. 'I just wanna go home.'

44

Lessons Learnt

My parents' greatest gift to their children, next to their unwavering love, was resilience. They knew how to let us make our own mistakes, which is easier said than done. In part, I think it was generational. That was the way it was done in the suburbs in the early nineties. But it was also personal. Here were two people who had left school early and lost their fathers at a young age. As young adults, they suffered more trauma: Dad had seen and heard men drown; Mum barely escaped death in a car accident. It explains why they didn't lecture me about my binge drinking as I neared the end of the school year. Quiet, stern words were offered not as condemnation but advice. But there was more to their resilience teaching. For eighteen years, I'd watched my folks show us how to pick ourselves up and keep going. It was in their language. We all make mistakes. No one's perfect. There's always tomorrow. Get back up and get on with it. It was also in their working lives. Mum's transition back to part-time work and then full-time school was a mountain to climb but she ascended it, then found a bigger mountain: keeping troubled kids safe. Up she went again. There was no glory for her in that position, nor did she seek it. 'Someone has to do it, why not me?' she would say. 'Those children need help.' She could never do enough.

Decades later, when Mum was told she had Parkinson's, the disease didn't stop her. For a long time, she was its conqueror, a warrior still.

Dad faced different demons. Physically, he had to manage back pain. But his nemesis must've been turning up for work, day after day, year after year, in jobs he was too good for. He drove trucks for much of my childhood, but he worked other jobs too. For a time, he built children's playgrounds. He also worked for the power tool company Skill. (Management gave him a box of merchandise. Jo, Steve, Kate and I were photographed wearing our 'Do it with Skill' T-shirts.) He worked briefly for Frankston Council. He flirted with starting his own handyman business and even had cards made up with his phone number on them. Nothing came of it. He had no experience in small business. But he had other talents, like drawing. He did a night course at Frankston TAFE, bought a drafting table, and started designing home extensions. Having helped my uncle Garry build our house, he did the same years later, putting up our shared holiday house in Phillip Island. Mum and Dad later bought old properties in Seaford and Frankston. Dad fixed them up, rented them out. He needed the security – he never earned superannuation and his salary was never high. Dad succeeded, and thrived, because of his intelligence, work ethic and partnership with Mum.

If Dad had been born into an educated family, he might well have been a barrister or a town planner. But would he have been happier and more productive? Would he have built homes and lives, and been as dearly loved by his children? I doubt it. A great deal of his strength came from the challenges he had to overcome to be a good father. He had little firsthand experience of how a father was supposed to act. He learnt everything on the job. Again, Mum helped him along, step by step.

Both my parents liked walking for exercise, and to clear their heads. They did it alone, with other people, or together. If they were absent for an hour or so near dusk, one of us kids would comment: 'Mum and Dad gone for a walk?' Every now and then I spotted them strolling down to the beach or back, holding hands like teenagers. It was their one show of public affection.

When I let my parents down, or didn't meet their expectations, there were no hysterics. If they gave me any grief, it was subtle: pity, avoidance or silence. One of Dad's favourite sayings was, 'Silence is the stern reply.'

45

Soundtrack of My Youth

In the final weeks of school, I decided to give up drinking. The Metro debacle weighed heavily on my mind, if not my liver. My abstinence lasted four weeks – I could hardly say no to a few beers the night before muck-up day.

It was a Thursday night in October. We went to Frankston's only Irish Bar, tucked in behind the Pancake Parlour on Nepean Highway. There was a band playing and the room seemed alive with the drumbeat. The cigarette smoke alone made me dizzy. All my mates were there from school. Not just Adam, Leigh and Doc. There was Cameron Milligan, Travis McQuirk, Matthew Higgins, Brian Dupas and half a dozen others. We'd been at high school together for six years. It would all end the next day. We slung our arms around each other to songs by Spin Doctors, 4 Non Blondes, Arrested Development, The Heights, Inner Circle, Janet Jackson, The Proclaimers, Ace of Base, and DJ Jazzy Jeff & The Fresh Prince. 'Boom! Shake the room'.

Adam, whose voice was the soundtrack of my youth, led the impromptu choir. We looked to him to set the standard. As usual, he closed his eyes and gave it everything. We all did. I felt rushes of freedom and happiness and love for my friends. We swore never to forget each other or the time we'd shared. I never broke that promise.

Adam and I started talking on the bar stools between the band's sets. I was nursing a bourbon and Coke, not tempted to skull it. For once, I was trying to make this high last. I didn't want the night to end.

'I think I'm gunna join a band,' Adam said.

'Which band?'

'Mercy Dash,' he said. 'The one that plays in Frankston. They've got regular gigs in the city.'

'Mate, you'll kill it. They got groupies?'

'I hope so.'

'Well, I'll be one of them. I'll be there every night.' And I would be. When Adam became a lead singer I was right up the front, dancing poorly. One of Mercy Dash's regular gigs was at Joey's, a small, dark bar in inner-city St Kilda, at 1am on Saturdays. I never missed a set.

'Cheers, mate, what about you?' He asked me if I thought I could make it to the AFL. The national draft was being held the following morning, broadcast on TV for the first time. I planned to watch it on a telly outside the principal's office, or in the staff room if they let me.

'Doubt it,' I said. I couldn't say it out loud, not even to Adam, but I still hoped my name might be called in the draft. Somebody at some club might have spotted something in me. My dream of playing AFL was still alive – just.

I told Adam I wanted to pursue journalism as a trade, or maybe plumbing. (Steve had helped me get an interview with the Gas & Fuel Corporation.)

The band started up again. They were belting out my favourite pub song of the day, 'I'm Too Sexy' by Right Said Fred. I whooped and hollered and charged back onto the dance floor along with everyone else. We didn't stop singing till last drinks, a little after midnight. I can't remember any girls from school being there that night, but they must have been because Adam went home with one of them – classic smoke bomb. When the lights came on, I couldn't find him.

46

Mucking Up

I can't say for sure how I ended up at school at two o'clock in the morning. But I do know that amid the euphoric haze of closing time at the Irish pub, muck-up day had something to do with it. By the time taxis were ordered, however, only three of us stayed the course. Everyone else went home.

There was Travis McQuirk, Matthew 'Higgo' Higgins and me. My drunken elation was ebbing as we staggered into the school grounds. The night air was warm. There were no stars in the sky. We got our bearings at the portable classrooms and headed for the oval. It was so quiet we could hear the frogs in the swamp.

'We've got about four hours,' Trav said. He was a cheery kid with a blond mullet. He was my age but looked about three years younger. Son of a single mum, he was naive, eager to please, and the least likely of any of my schoolmates to get in trouble. I was surprised he was with us at this hour, but he was close to Higgo. Higgo was the more daring of the two, a tall larrikin who pretended not to care about anything, except his beloved Carlton Football Club. He was no academic, but I reckoned he was sharper than he let on.

'Why don't we go into the hall, play basketball,' Higgo was

saying. 'We can get out the mini tramp.' The idea appealed. Slam-dunking with the aid of those trampolines was my favourite way to pass the time in Phys Ed classes.

'Reckon it'll be open?' Trav said.

'We can find a way in,' Higgo said.

No one asked the obvious question: What happens if we get caught?

The gym hall had at least three entrances, including a side door with a porthole window. Trav and Higgo tried to smash the round glass with rocks and bricks but it was too thick. We needed a heavier projectile.

'Let's try this,' I said, hoisting a metal fire hydrant cover. Shaped like a witch's hat but with a flat red top, it was the perfect battering ram. 'They really should bolt these things down.'

I rushed at the window, hurling the hydrant cover. It made a glancing blow and bounced back at me onto the concrete steps with a clang. The boys laughed.

'That's one tough window,' Higgo said.

Trav suggested we give up.

'Nup,' I said. 'I reckon I can break it.'

My second throw was more accurate. The makeshift battering ram smashed the glass, leaving a jagged hole just big enough for Trav to climb through. He opened the door from the inside, one hand dripping blood from the shards still embedded in the door.

'It's nothin,' he said, cradling his hand in his shirt. 'Come on in, lads.'

It was darker inside than out, but I knew my way around. We were in a corridor near the backstage area, and music department. As my eyes adjusted, I could see drums, keyboards and guitar cases lying around. I thought of my days as a budding musician. Back in Year 7, I'd started learning the saxophone because I'd seen Rob Lowe do it in *St Elmo's Fire*. I even joined the band. It was full on. We played concerts at Moorabbin Town Hall. In performances, I wore slacks for the first time, with a white collared shirt. I loved learning to read and play music, including the classic 'Arthur's Theme'. I liked the way new reeds softened under my tongue, the way my fingers eventually found their places on the gold buttons, how I improved from week to week. I liked seeing myself as more than a sports-loving boofhead. Then one day a much older student mocked me for carrying my instrument around the playground in its coffin-like case. 'Hey geek, I bet you that thing is bigger than you.' The criticism made no sense, but other big kids laughed along. I wanted to drop the case and run. Instead, I slunk away. Next day, I told my music teacher Mr Seymour the saxophone just wasn't for me. He looked at me with genuine pity. 'What a shame, man,' he said. 'You could've been a good musician.' Six years on, here I was. I wondered how good I'd be, if only I'd ignored the schoolyard critics.

'This way,' Higgo was saying. He was already on the basketball court.

It was black as a cave. I could hear Trav scrambling for a light switch. As far as I could tell I was somewhere around the halfcourt line. Of all my memories of that night, it's that moment in that dark void that stays with me most vividly. The Pearl Jam song 'Jeremy' was still ringing in my ears from the pub, and I was mouthing the chorus.

I was suddenly exhausted, with echoes of the night urging me to sleep. I thought about lying down on the hardwood floor.

'What's up there?' Higgo called out.

A small, red light was flashing in a corner of the high ceiling.

'Oh, shit,' I heard myself say. It was a silent alarm. It would be going off somewhere, alerting security. I still had too much bourbon in my blood to be panicking. I felt more irritation than dread. 'Time to fuck off.'

We fumbled blindly for a side door, unbolted it and stepped out into the night. The door slammed shut behind us. In front of us, a man in uniform was leaning on the fence outside the principal's office. He was staring straight at us.

'G'day gentlemen,' the security guard said. He was middle aged, with a warm smile.

'G'day,' I said. 'School's hiring guards these days? What for?'

The guard took a step closer. 'The principal wanted to make sure there was no trouble on muck-up day,' he said. 'I don't expect any. Maybe some eggs and flour, that sort of stuff. Just kids being kids.'

Higgo was nodding enthusiastically. 'That makes sense,' he said.

I tried not to laugh at his overacting.

'Where have you fellas come from?' the guard said. It didn't sound like an accusation.

'Just passing through,' I said. 'Been a big night out. We're going home.'

I started to walk away but he stepped in front of me.

'Sounds like you've had a good time,' he said. 'You haven't seen anyone hanging around the hall, have you?'

'The gym?' Trav said. 'Nah. Not us.'

The guard looked at Trav's bleeding hand. Trav stuck it in his pocket.

'We haven't seen anyone,' I said. 'Why?'

'Oh, one of the alarms went off. It's probably nothing. But, listen, do me a favour, just hang around for a few minutes longer would you?'

I heard the cop cars arrive before I saw them – a roar of engines, skidding tyres and slamming doors. I saw lights flashing red and blue on the stunned faces of Trav and Higgo as I was knocked to the ground. There was a knee on my neck and my right cheek was squashed against the footpath.

'We didn't do anything,' I said.

'Shut the fuck up,' said the cop on top of me. He was handcuffing me behind my back, way too tight.

The cops frogmarched me to a waiting car. The security guard watched me go, still wearing the same warm smile. I admired him, and still do. There was no boast in the expression he gave me. He was just doing his job.

Just like in all the police movies I'd ever seen, an officer shoved my head down as I went into the back seat. We sped out onto the highway, north towards the city.

The officer behind the wheel asked me my name.

Our eyes met in the rear-view mirror. He was young, and angry.

'Paul.'

'Paul, sir,' he corrected. 'Last name?'

'Kennedy.'

'Kennedy, *sir*,' he said. 'You call me sir, do you understand?'

His partner, who was maybe a few years older, said nothing. He frowned out the window as we crossed the mouth of Patterson River. Port Phillip Bay was serene in the distance.

I didn't understand the angry cop's need for authority. I was already shackled. At first I felt pissed off at him. Who was he to speak to me like that? It had been a long night, a long year. Not much had gone the way I'd planned. In fact, most things had turned to shit. Adulthood was hard and I was scared, always bloody scared. The cop fumed and waited for my response.

'I don't think I want to call you sir,' I said.

The car skidded to a thumping halt. With no free hands to steady myself I crashed into the front seat. We were in the middle of the highway. The furious driver twisted in his seat to glare at me. I could tell he wanted to hit me. After a brief, ridiculous stare-off, he turned back to the wheel and we took off faster than before.

We screeched into a car park two or three minutes later. It was the Chelsea Police Station. The officers dragged me out by one of my elbows and led me to a bungalow-type building. I heard one of them call it a holding cell.

'How long?' I said as they shoved me inside, still handcuffed, and slammed the door. 'I get a phone call, don't I?'

I heard fading footsteps, and another door slam. They hadn't left any lights on. I was in pitch dark again.

'Anyone in here?' I said. Silence, save for the lapping of the tide a block away. I rolled over onto my side, my head on the cold floor. I was glad to know I'd soon be asleep.

47

Any Questions?

———————

I was dazed and confused when the cops dragged me out of the cell and into the station. The outside world was dim and grey, the morning light still a way off. They dumped me in a seat in an interview room. And they read me my rights. The young cop no longer seemed angry. His older partner was more relaxed, too. They sat opposite me.

'Any questions?'

'Yeah.' My voice was broken. I felt all but sober. My wrists were raw from the steel cuffs. There was a tape recorder on the table. 'When do I get to make a call?'

'Who do you wanna call?'

'My mum.'

'The number?' the younger cop said. He picked up a phone, his dialling finger hovering.

'Nah, I don't want you to call her,' I said. 'I'll call her. She'll be scared if she hears your voice first.'

The cop shook his head. 'That's not how it works. You've been arrested. You're not calling the shots. I'll speak to your mum, tell her what's happened and then you can talk. It's up to you. It's your phone call. You don't have to have one.'

He held up the receiver as a question mark.

'Or,' his partner said, 'we can get on with the interview and you can call her later, mate.'

'Yeah, don't worry about it,' I said. I had an image of Mum's panicked face in my mind. I couldn't stand it. 'Let's get on with it.'

The young cop started setting up the cassette recorder. 'Your mates told us everything so don't bother bullshitting us,' he said.

I wondered whether Higgo and Trav would have folded so easily. I told myself they wouldn't have. I felt defiant. My plan was to deny, deny. The truth, in my foggy mind, was that we didn't even go near the gym. We were just good citizens helping the security guard when the cops rolled up all heavy handed. Then I remembered Trav's sliced up hand. His blood all over the crime scene. Would they do DNA tests? Fuck. Or fingerprints? I should have worn gloves. We all should have.

The little wheels in the tape started turning. The young cop read my rights again and stated the time. 'Do you agree the time is now 4.39am?'

I nodded.

'You have to speak,' the older cop said. 'So the tape picks it up.'

I leaned over the recorder. 'I agree.'

These formalities jerked me into reality. I was in too deep to talk my way out. Surrender was my only hope. The cops questioned me about my night and I told them everything. The look on their faces as I explained how we broke into the gym told me they weren't used to such willing confessions.

I found out later why it was so satisfying for them. They hadn't spoken to Higgo or Trav at all. They didn't know anything about us, or our crime. My two mates weren't eighteen yet, so they couldn't be treated like me – they were dozing in another room.

When I told the cops that our only intention in the gym was to shoot hoops until school started for our last day, the mood of the room changed. The young cop looked at the older cop. Their shoulders slumped. They were like a couple of big-game fishermen who'd reeled in an old boot. I was no one's white whale. They hadn't cracked a break-and-enter syndicate. I actually felt a bit bad for them.

'So you weren't trying to steal anything?' the older cop said.

'Nah, it's our school. We go there.'

With a rueful smile on his face, the younger cop started writing something in pencil on a serviette. He slid the note across the table while asking me another question.

'Why did you break into the school hall?'

He was pointing at the note. He wanted me to read aloud.

Bewildered, I squinted at the words. I couldn't read the cop's writing. His penmanship was poor, even allowing for the flimsy paper.

'I can't read that,' I said.

The policemen lifted their hands in exasperation. The young cop actually slapped his forehead with his palm and mouthed the words, 'fuck me'. He sighed and leaned back in, pointed at the serviette. Not wanting to disappoint him again, I took another look and concentrated hard. Finally, I made out the words.

'Oh,' I said, clearing my throat to recite the note. 'I was drunk.'

The interview was over. The older cop gave me a weary thumbs up.

I agreed the time was what they said it was. The recorder was turned off. I was given one of the tapes (I still have it) and a sheet of paper noting my arrest details. The younger cop said he'd talk to his sergeant and work out what I'd be charged with.

'Wanna call your mum?' he said.

'Not now,' I said.

'We've contacted your principal,' he said. 'He wants you to go to school and speak to him there.'

'Okay, thanks.' I was still clutching the serviette. 'Want this back?'

'Keep it as a reminder,' he said. 'And don't be so stupid next time.'

Higgo, Trav and I were reunited in a side street off Nepean Highway, near the long Chelsea shopping strip. The sun was climbing into the sky, hurting my eyes. We caught a train back to Carrum, closest to school, and ran past a ticket inspector on the platform. (None of us had change to pay the fare.) We started laughing and couldn't stop. Freedom felt good.

48

Unwanted

An hour later, I was sitting on a low, red-cushioned seat outside the principal's office. Again, I'd been separated from Trav and Higgo. My head throbbed. I ached for sleep. Word must have travelled fast about our arrest. Students I didn't even know kept coming by to look at me. My mind was turning to possible consequences, a criminal record chief among them. My chances of getting a cadetship or apprenticeship now looked grim; my faint hope of an AFL lifeline fainter still.

Which reminded me. It was about ten o'clock. The TV was right there in the foyer. I changed the channel to the AFL national draft. I watched on wistfully, with an ember of hope in my heart. I knew that if I heard my name called, it was far more likely to be the principal calling it.

The draft produced a lot of a names I knew from our Under 18 competition. Justin Murphy (Central). Glenn Gorman (Geelong). Angelo Lekkas (Northern). The Stingrays had a boy drafted to St Kilda at number twenty-five. His name was Clinton Shaw. I'd never met him, although I'd heard he was a top endurance athlete from the Mornington Peninsula who'd missed our season through injury. I doubted he was a better player than our best onballers,

Dean Watson and Brett Anthony. Our next draftee was All-Australian full back Mick Prentice. He was going to Melbourne. At some point I stopped listening for my name and started wondering which club would recruit Smithy. Finally, I heard it.

'With pick 61, Sydney Swans select Shayne Smith, Southern Stingrays.'

Of course the Swans wanted him. In one of the reserves games he played for them, he kicked five goals against Essendon – a boy dominating a men's competition.

Jeff White didn't get picked up in the 1993 draft. (He would be selected by Fremantle the following year. He went number one, the best prospect in Australian football.)

The AFL telecast ended. Watto, BA and our skipper Benny Delarue all went undrafted. Watto was the biggest surprise. He was the league best and fairest, for God's sake. What more could he do? Cruelly, almost every club had told him they were considering taking him. If he couldn't make the grade, I was no chance.

The truth was hard to swallow. The fact was I'd failed because of the mistakes I'd made, and listening to the draft outside the principal's office was a fitting reminder – one final humiliation. I was undrafted, unwanted and going nowhere. All I was, and all I willed myself to be since I started with plastic balls in the yard at Puckapunyal, was now nothing more than a silly fantasy.

Thinking about it that morning, with no more lies to tell and no one to hear them, I could see my failings all too clearly. Fear had got me. In the back of my mind, I was so worried about not being good enough to make the AFL, I stopped trying as hard as I needed to. Better to be cavalier than dedicated. Go for a drink with the boys, it won't matter. I figured no one would be able to see through my recklessness. What an excuse. Too bloody scared. Weak as piss, I was.

'He's ready to see you now,' the office secretary said.

I took a deep breath, walked into the principal's office, and got expelled. There were no questions, no answers, no way out.

'You will never set foot in this school again,' the principal told me. He spoke without a trace of compassion. 'Get your things and go home.' He said the police were considering charging me with serious offences.

I felt like I should have been crying. But no tears came. A numbing disappointment overwhelmed all other emotions. I'd let down everyone who thought I was better than this. I imagined my parents' faces when they found out, and I felt sick. But most of all, I felt tired – tired of being me.

In my pounding head I could barely comprehend what it all might mean. Criminal record aside, I was facing the prospect of not being able to do my final exams. Would I have to repeat the whole year at another school?

I slunk away through the back gate. I didn't see Adam or any of the other boys, or Mrs Mac. I didn't want to. Not until I could somehow fix what I had broken.

49

Apologies

———————

I tried to hide for a while after my expulsion.

I got to know the inside of my bedroom again. I read. I listened to music. I did not look at myself in the mirror. I cried a few times.

When my hangover receded, and I could see more clearly the dream of playing AFL was dead, I grieved for it. Falling short of my ambition wasn't the worst part. I felt like I'd lost a dear companion. What dream did I have left? All my days I'd wanted to be a footballer. Now, nobody would ever come to watch me play; no one would ever know my name. I felt ridiculous for spending so much time fancying I could make the big time. Why didn't someone tell me I was a dickhead for trying?

Eventually, I slept without waking every hour. I went to bed early to be with my unconscious thoughts, hoping they could give me some direction.

I decided to write letters to those I felt I'd let down. It was the only way I could say sorry for being such a disappointment. I wrote them and rewrote them to get them right. The letters carried not only my apology but everything I had and felt and knew and feared.

Mum and Dad replied to their letters by saying they forgave me. They did it without delay or drama. Their love kept me from falling to pieces.

Days passed. Then I received a two-page letter on floral-framed paper from Mrs Mac. It read:

Dear Paul,

Thank you for your letter. I hope that by now you're feeling a little more comfortable with yourself. Believe it or not, Thursday night was not the worst thing to happen in the history of the school. You're human, with lots of good and a few bad points, but the good far outweigh the bad, so ease up on yourself a bit. You've obviously learnt from the experience and that's enough. It would be nice to have the ability to go back and change the past but we can't. We just have to get on with the now.

The most important thing for me in your letter was your thanks for the friendship and for this year. That means a lot to me. I've enjoyed getting to know you more the more I've taught you, and to know that is reciprocated really matters to me. I've teased you a fair amount during the year and you've taken it really well. Class and the chats... outside of it were always fun.

I'm not expressing myself very clearly, which is no advertisement for my abilities as an English teacher. I guess I'm just trying to say that it doesn't matter what you've done or what you may do in the future, you will always matter to me.

Be good and try to be happy. See you soon.

P.S. I really like the fact that you've looked up to me. Coming from someone 6'2" to someone 5'2", it makes me smile. But I do appreciate the sentiment.

P.P.S Did Adam get caught throwing eggs on cars? If not, there's an amusing story circulating about him.

Mrs Mac's letter gave me permission to start breathing again, and start thinking about what I might do to salvage something from the year. I studied for my exams, just in case I was allowed to take them. Also, I decided to take a journalism cadetship test in the city.

Another letter arrived in the mail. It was a school newsletter. Under a headline 'Student Behaviour, End of School Activities', it detailed three students being charged by police. 'The College Council has expressed great concern at this incident', it reported. Attached to the newsletter was a note from the principal outlining the cost of repairing the door and window I broke. It was almost a thousand dollars. The principal added, 'Accordingly I would like you to pay your share of $329.00 at the earliest date possible.'

Given the circumstance, I thought it was a very polite letter.

50

Nothing to Lose

A week later I was standing among a hundred or so clear-eyed teenagers in a narrow hallway in Melbourne. It was the RMIT building, fourth level. Each of us was carrying a pen, pencil and rubber. When the door in front of us opened we'd head in to take the *Herald Sun* cadetship examination. All the kids around me, some high-school students and a lot more university graduates, wanted to be journalists. I wasn't so sure. But here I was. I looked for people I recognised and was pleased to find none. Getting bored, I started perving at the girls, trying to decide who was the prettiest. Some of them were wearing summer dresses. There was a girl beside me I'd adjudged to be in the top three. I was surprised to find myself chatting to her, and even more surprised that I was relaxed about it. Perhaps it was because she didn't know anything about me.

'What do you reckon they'll test us on?' I said.

'I was told it was in two parts, writing some sort of essay and then general knowledge,' she said.

The girl had long, red-brown hair, brown eyes, whiter than white teeth.

I asked her what school she went to. I didn't recognise the

name. She told me it was in Toorak. I assumed this made her smart. I decided to sit next to her.

'Where's your school?' she asked. When I told her and then explained where it was, she seemed unimpressed. Or was I imagining it?

'That's a long way to come,' she said. 'Did you drive in or catch the train?'

I lied and told her I drove. Mum and Dad had given me a lift. They'd gone for lunch somewhere along Swanston Street.

My oldies had been heartbroken by the whole muck-up day fiasco. I saw disappointment and exhaustion and pity in the way they looked at me. But there were no heart-to-hearts; no yelling or screaming. When I was hurting, they let me hurt, without letting me suffer. They told me I needed to turn things around. And, rightly or wrongly, they hugged me tighter in disgrace than they did in moments of jubilation. All children should be so fortunate to be given such care.

When the door opened for our exam to start, I was glad. I was all out of small talk. My new friend and I got separated, and I ended up sitting at a table next to a young man about my age. He carried his writing tools admirably in an unmarked pencil case.

For the writing test we were given a sheet of paper with details of an accident. It read like a police report. Our task was to write a news story based on the available facts. I wrote four or five paragraphs, keeping my sentences short. When I finished, I looked around and saw most of the other wannabe reporters still going. I wondered whether I'd made a mistake by being too succinct.

The general knowledge test was tougher, at least for me. Aside from Frankston crime stories, I still only read about footy and cricket. I tried to cheat by copying answers from the competent-looking fellow next to me but when he covered his work with his forearm, I was stuffed. One of the questions was: 'Who owns News Limited?' I didn't know it was Rupert Murdoch – I'd never heard of him. I didn't even know News Limited owned the *Herald* and *Weekly Times*, where I was applying for a job. I wrote my answer as, 'Oprah Winfrey'. I gave the same answer for subsequent questions as jokes, or more accurately: white flags.

When our time was up, we were told that only twelve of us would be selected for the next stage. A panel of editorial staff would then interview those dozen applicants.

I raised my hand. 'How many cadetships do you give?' I didn't want to leave without knowing the odds.

'Only six.'

I noticed some furrowed brows.

Afterwards, Mum and Dad were waiting for me outside.

'How'd you go, mate?' Dad said.

I shrugged.

'I'm sure it wasn't that bad,' Mum said. 'Anyway, consider it good practice for the future.'

Statewide high school testing was held the following week. While my principal hadn't overturned my expulsion, he had allowed for me to do my exams at neighbouring Mordialloc-Chelsea Secondary College. I could still get my VCE certificate. Higgo and Trav were in the same situation.

Intent on making amends by finishing with decent grades, I stayed up late every night studying. Along the way, I fell in love with the taste of instant coffee.

Mum gave me a ride to my first exam. It made her late for work and her resentment was obvious. I caught the train to the rest of them. Students at Mordialloc-Chelsea studied me with suspicion. I saw Trav and Higgo around but we didn't stop to talk.

For my final English Lit assignment, I had to write a follow-up to the short story *Southern Skies* by David Malouf. The story was about a boy coming of age in Brisbane, and his relationship to a family friend called The Professor. I adored the way Malouf presented the world through the boy's loss of innocence. The story ended with the Professor masturbating the boy while he studied the stars through the old man's telescope. I considered the Professor an irredeemable grub, at best. But my task wasn't to judge Malouf's characters. Instead, I had to write a two-page sequel. I turned the story on my life, examining drinking, hangovers, sex, sport, youthful disappointment and hope. Not sure whether I deserved it, but I got an A.

Surprisingly, I excelled in Legal Studies more than English or Lit. I got an A plus in the last exam of the year, which involved explaining the merits of jury trials as opposed to judge-only trials. (I was told years later that my Legal Studies teacher, the charismatic Mr O'Brien, started using me as an example when lecturing his students about commitment: 'When you finally put in the work, you get your rewards.')

Adam was my biggest help during this time. Between studying, I kept popping around to his place. He enjoyed hearing about me being handcuffed, while condemning my actions as 'fucking stupid'. I asked him whether he got caught throwing eggs at cars, as Mrs Mac had alluded to in her letter. He denied it. I knew he wouldn't go egging without me. He completed his exams with a minimum of effort, dreaming of his future in music.

'What are you doing about footy? he said.

'Probably play for Seaford next year,' I told him. 'With Steve and his mates.'

He was unimpressed. 'That's not like you,' he said. 'I've stuck up for you. When people told me you couldn't play footy at the higher level I said you could, and then you did.'

'Not very well,' I said.

'But you did it,' he said. 'You always adapt. Don't give up.'

51

Fond Farewells

The Stingrays held a presentation night and vote count. It was at the social rooms where we'd trained all year. We had dinner and watched a highlights video. Then Hutchy read out the votes for best players from the start of the year until the end. After a promising start, I finished sixth. BA and Watto were second and third, behind the winner Smithy.

I was sorry our year had finished the way it had, but most of all I was just sad it finished. I said goodbye to my teammates for the final time. We promised to keep in touch.

Then it was school's turn, with an end-of-year dinner for Year 12s. I assumed I wouldn't be allowed to attend, until I heard it was to be held off campus – at nearby Bonbeach High School. I bought a red paisley tie and a green shirt for the occasion. Adam and Leigh also wore ties. Doc went with a navy blazer and open-necked shirt. He looked smooth. That's how he stays in my memory. I never saw him again after that night. How easily good friends can lose each other after the routine of school falls away.

On the night, the teachers stood up on stage and gave awards to all the graduates. Parents and family friends were in the audience. Mrs Mac and Mrs Reg read out my citation. For a few laughs they noted how I endlessly injected football references into works of literature, rearranged tributes to former principals (the BBQ plaque) and 'made my mark on end-of-year traditions'. No one mentioned my arrest. I smiled sheepishly.

I was pleased to hear my literature classmate Jane Prentice won one of two awards for outstanding academic achievement, equivalent to our best and fairest.

Afterwards, we all posed for photographs, breaking into groups to smile for the camera.

When we got our yearbooks, I saw that someone had drawn up a list of awards in the back page. Some of the categories were peculiar. I won some athletic-themed awards. And, regrettably, Most Chauvinistic. Adam was chosen by his peers to have Best Personality. He'd been the most popular kid in our classes since he was five. It was a thirteen-year unmatchable stretch of fun-loving kind-heartedness. Doc won Most Sexy. I wasn't surprised to hear I missed out on Most Ambitious. That award went to a boy called Brett George, who also took out Most Likely to Succeed and Best Floppy Disk Worker. Brett later moved to a curious-sounding town called Silicon Valley.

We signed each other's yearbooks, not knowing that, in many cases, they were the last words we'd offer each other. For me, Louise King wrote, 'All the best, love Lou.' My heart skipped a long-lost beat.

Some of the students went out for drinks. I, for once, went straight home.

The next day I got a letter from the *Herald* and *Weekly Times*. 'Congratulations! You've made it through to the next round ...'

For the interview at the HWT building I wore the same green

shirt and red tie from the Year 12 dinner. It was the only formal wear I owned.

I felt terribly insecure as I was ushered into a seat in front of a three-member panel at a long table.

They began by lowering my expectations. 'We just want you to be aware that while we might pick one or two high school leavers, we prefer university graduates. So, you're up against it, but you've made it this far.'

Then came the better news. They were actually impressed by my news writing. 'It was one of the best we got back. Didn't waste words, really nailed the news angle. Fantastic.'

They were less impressed with my general knowledge efforts. At the mention of my answers, one of the panel members screwed up her face.

'Oprah Winfrey, eh?' another one of them said. 'We had a good laugh at that.'

'To be perfectly blunt,' the panel chair said, 'your general knowledge is one of the worst we've ever come across. Do you read newspapers?'

'Just the sport section,' I said.

'How do you write so well if you don't read widely?' one of them said. 'Is it natural?'

'Some of it,' I said. 'My parents have always encouraged me, and I've had some great teachers.'

'Ah, yes,' the chair said. 'We've heard from them.' I'd presented the panel no fewer than six references from my teachers, who generously typed up letters on school letterhead. None of them mentioned that I'd been expelled.

Mrs Reg wrote a long reference, taking up the whole page.

'Paul has a wide circle of friends and is a popular, friendly student. His humour and fun-loving attitude have helped to make, not only classes, but school social events enjoyable for all concerned.'

Mrs Mac went further on the social referencing. 'Paul has been a student in classes I have taken out of the school on excursions and camps. I have observed him at more socially oriented school functions such as the Senior Ball, Year 12 Dinner… His behaviour has always been exemplary.'

It's possible she was overcompensating. The panel chair read out the last line and chuckled. 'Well, it's good to know you're well behaved when you get out and about.'

Given journalists are renowned big drinkers, I'm not surprised this tickled them. But, at the time, I had no context to interpret the comment. I genuinely thought they were laughing because they knew about my trouble with the police. It threw me off. For the rest of the interview, I was suspicious and standoffish.

'Well,' the chair said when we were done. 'We'll let you know.'

I wasn't surprised when the panel wrote to me a week later telling me I'd missed out on the cadetship. Better luck next year.

52

Where Does the Water Go?

With school finished, I needed to earn a living. Steve arranged for me to do some labouring with one of the senior blokes at the Seaford Football Club. Frank was his name. He was built like a tank and seemed to love what he did. I admired him straight away. On my first day Mum dropped me off at Frank's house at five o'clock in the morning. It was exciting – a real job. Frank drove a F100 with one hand, while drinking a cuppa from a mug. I made a note to do that when I got my first car.

We arrived at a hot, dusty worksite in St Albans, on the other side of the city. It seemed like another world. Frank handed me a shovel and told me to dig a trench. I went at it with a velocity designed to impress my boss. Problem was the ground was rock hard. I could barely break the surface. By midday I'd hardly achieved anything, save for tearing the skin off my hands.

'Mate, you should've worn gloves,' said Frank.

On a lunch break I sat in a shed with one of Frank's sub-contractors, a funny bloke called Yogi. I kept looking at Yogi's hand because he had a couple of fingers missing. Later than afternoon, Frank asked me if I'd ever used an angle grinder. I hadn't even heard of one. Frank said not to worry, it was easy to use. He got me to cut between two rows of bricks, for reasons never explained to me. I was careful not to cut off my fingers and end up like Yogi.

Working with Frank was satisfying, to a point. I lost track of time for hours each day. Digging trenches became my favourite task, blisters and all. I refused to wear gloves, as no other workers had them on; they seemed to be dismissed as a concession of weakness. I didn't want to draw that sort of attention. I put up with the sore hands and wielded a power tool properly for the first time in my life. I could do it while letting my mind run free. I'd started daydreaming again, only with more breadth. I still imagined myself playing professional sport, a hard habit to break, but I was also back to fantasising about writing books.

A million whims aside, there are only two things I've ever wanted to be in this world – a footballer player and a writer.

I still went out on Saturday nights but curtailed my drinking. Outside The Grand one weekend, I saw a girl I knew. Her name was Jamie Taylor. We'd got friendly at a party earlier in the year. I'd worked up the courage to talk to her. Though we'd grown up in the same estate, we hadn't crossed paths like that before. But when she invited me to a ball at her private school, my bravery failed me. I knocked her back because I was too worried about being an outsider in her world.

It was good to see her again. Jamie and I made small talk, went inside, and kept chatting on the stools at the bar. She asked me about my footy. I asked her about her gymnastics. We talked about growing up so close, without ever getting to know each other. We sat there a long time. People came by. I introduced her to other friends. Jamie teased me for knowing almost everyone in the pub. I made a few cracks about her going to a la-di-da school and forgetting about her roots. Eventually we left our friends, and even gave Uncle Vic's a miss. I hailed a cab. We cuddled in the back seat. The taxi pulled up outside her house and I asked if I could come in, just for a bit.

'We've gotta be quiet though,' she said. 'Don't wake my parents.'

I tipped the cabbie before Jamie could change her mind. I was in a good mood, having not drunk as much as I usually did. I felt lighter; carefree in a good way. Is this what I'd been missing all along?

We held hands as we crept through the kitchen. The more Jamie tried to stay quiet the more she laughed. 'Come on, this way.' Safe inside her room, we kissed on the bed. I felt comfortable, as if I'd been there before, which was strange because I'd never been near her house, not even when we were kids. At some point Jamie quizzed me about her school formal. 'Why didn't you come with me?'

I was hoping she wouldn't ask. 'Dunno. I'm sorry I didn't.'

She wasn't mad. She was curious. 'If you liked me, and now I know you do, why wouldn't you say yes?' She poked me in the chest.

'Dunno.'

It was dark in the room, but I could see her pretty face from the street light outside.

'Tell me why,' she said.

'I was scared,' I blurted. 'I didn't know anyone at your school. I find those situations a bit awkward.'

'You would've been with me, ya duffer,' she said. 'I wouldn't have left you alone.'

'Sorry,' I said. 'It's something I've gotta fix.'

'I wanted to see you in a tuxedo.' Then her face became serious. 'It's okay to admit you're sensitive about stuff. You're a softie at heart. That's what I like about you.'

We started kissing again, rearranging each other's clothes without having sex. I stroked her hair while she started falling asleep. 'You'll make a good boyfriend one day,' she said. It was a compliment, not an offer. I nodded off after she did. An hour or so later she shook me awake. 'You'd better go.'

I snuck out of her room and out of her house. Our shared estate, the one I'd known when it was no more than a clearing of mud and fresh bitumen, was still cosy to me. Dawn wasn't far off. I walked a couple of blocks to get home.

I was never with Jamie again. Part of this had to do with chance: I never saw her back at the Frankston pubs. Also, I didn't have a car to take her on a date, so I never felt bold enough to call her up. Mostly, I wondered whether she'd like me as much if she got to know me better. Best to not risk it. We had a good night together and I could leave it there. Later, I heard she moved to Queensland.

When summer came around again in December, Adam and I went to the beach to jump off the pier. It had been saved. It was just the same as always. But we weren't. We felt like we were getting too old for it. I stopped diving from the railings, in case I misjudged a landing and broke my neck.

A job interview with Leader Newspapers turned out to be a bust, or at least it felt like that at the time. It was a ten-minute meeting with the Southern Division Editor, Tom Wiles. I asked him for a cadetship and he asked me what experience I had in newsrooms.

'None,' I said.

'Well, I can't employ someone with no experience,' he said. 'How do I know you're serious about journalism?'

Exasperated, I answered him with a question of mine. 'How do I get experience if you don't give me a job?'

'That's not my problem. Go away and get some experience and I'm happy to hear from you again down the track.'

So, plumbing it was. I figured I could ride Steve's coattails to get an apprenticeship with the Gas & Fuel. My brother had got his ticket after four years of training. He was now fully qualified and had impressed plenty of people along the way.

My apprenticeship interview was in one of the brown brick towers in Flinders Street, about a hundred metres from the HWT building, where I really wanted to be. Since my cadetship rejection, I'd started yearning to write stories in that grand, mysterious place.

I reckon I almost had the apprenticeship in the bag before the interviewee, an honest, friendly man, asked me one last question. We were standing up, shaking hands. I'd half turned to leave the room.

'Just before you go,' he said, 'where does household water go?'

'Pardon me?' I said.

'Where does the water go? For example, if it goes down the drain in your kitchen sink. Where does it go from there?'

I was stumped. 'Ah, well that's obvious …'

'Yes, where?'

'You mean into the pipes?'

'What pipes?'

'Kitchen pipes.'

'Okay, kitchen pipes, call them that,' he said. 'Then where does it go? The water. It's down the sink …'

'… into the pipes?'

'Yes? And?'

'Actually,' I said. My shoulders sagged. I was sick of pretending. 'I'm buggered if I know. Is that a problem?'

We both started laughing.

'What do you really want to do?' he said. 'Because I don't think it's plumbing.'

'No idea,' I said. I wish I knew that smart man's name, so I could thank him for his honesty and kindness.

'Well good luck with whatever you do,' he said.

Soon after, the Frankston Serial Killer was sentenced to life for the murder of Elizabeth Stevens, Debbie Fream and Natalie Russell. He pleaded not guilty to the attempted murder of the woman outside the soccer club, which seemed wrong to me. Outside the court, defence barrister Brian Cash said his client was 'very frightened' of being attacked while serving his punishment. I was pleased. He deserved to be fearful. In sentencing, Supreme Court Justice Frank Vincent told the murderer: 'For many, you are the fear that quickens their steps as they walk alone, or causes a parent to look anxiously at the clock when a child is late. I suspect that you will never fully comprehend why this should be so, as, for reasons which we do not understand, you are not one of us.'

53

Laughing Gear

The year was all but done, which was a relief. I was eager to hop off this bloody rollercoaster. Only Christmas remained.

At eighteen, I didn't care so much for Christmas as an event. The Santa goosebumps, even memories of his presence, were long gone. And I was an aeon away from becoming a parent and rediscovering the magic that gets sprinkled twice on a lucky lifetime. But I still cherished the family time, even though it had a different energy now. Five out of six of us were adults. Jo had finished college. Steve was a qualified plumber. Little Katie was seventeen; she only had one year left at school.

Mum and Dad had announced they were planning to foster children during the holidays (called Holiday Hosting). The idea of not having kids in the house was frightening to them, I suppose. They had gone through a governmental interviewing program, which included psychological profiling. They each had a six-page dossier, describing their strengths and weaknesses as parents, among other things. I read these with interest: Mum describing Dad as 'quiet and considerate'; Dad describing Mum as 'friendly, good sense of humour, proud, tolerant to a point and then assertive'. Part of the questionnaire asked them about their plans for the future. Both mentioned they would like to travel. They'd already started eyeing off places to go around the world. Dad wrote: 'For ourselves I would like some more variation in life, peace, good health and eventually lots of grandchildren.'

After Christmas lunch, I made plans to catch up with Adam. There was an impromptu party happening. One of the girls from school was having people over. We caught a lift there. Our days of walking to parties and singing songs along the way were history.

There were a lot of schoolmates at the party, a mixture of boys and girls – or men and women as we were now. In a way, this felt like our real high-school ending. No speeches, awards or grown-ups watching over us. No angst. Nothing pending. Just friends who knew many of us would be going separate ways after this.

I was stretched out on a lounge, holding a stubbie but barely sipping it. Adam was beside me, holding court, telling jokes. Others gathered around, drawn in by his warmth.

On the spot, a bunch of us decided we'd drive to Queensland the next day – celebrate New Year's Eve at Surfers Paradise. Cameron Milligan volunteered his car for the odyssey. A week earlier I'd received a two-hundred-dollar cheque from St Kilda Football Club, as payment for my two games in July. It'd come in handy for petrol and food up north.

'It'll take us two days to get there,' someone said.

'Who cares? Let's just go.'

'Let's leave tonight,' said Adam.

'Righto,' I said. 'We'll head off at midnight.'

For the first time that whole year I felt entirely free, and not one bit lonely or afraid.

Adam cracked a gag that, for the life of me, I can't remember.

I started laughing so wildly I couldn't stop. My whole body got in on it. I started shaking, almost convulsing. I doubled over, sat up straight, doubled over again. He was laughing too. Tears were pouring down our cheeks. It felt so good to be out of control in a healthy way. My fit lasted about two minutes. The others were staring at me in amazement. The party's host, Melissa, said, 'I've never seen you laugh like that. In fact, I don't even think I've seen you laugh out loud.'

I was taken aback. 'Shit, really?' Was my mask of bravado fitted so tightly all these years? I explained that I was feeling more relaxed than usual.

'Well, I like this side of you,' Melissa said.

'Thanks.'

Everything I feared at the start of the year had come to pass. I was nowhere near where I set out to be. But I was just as happy as I had been back when I was a little kid riding around the streets drinking the rain.

I was among friends. I had so much to look forward to. I can see that now. That's why I was laughing so hard.

Epilogue

In 1994, the serial killer successfully argued for a lesser sentence – thirty years' minimum. He could walk free by 2023. Natalie Russell's parents, Carmel and Brian, who still live in Frankston, want the state to prevent this release. They're not alone. For so many, the grief still runs deep.

Every year, on the anniversary of their daughter's death, Carmel and Brian visit the path between the golf courses where Natalie was found. It's been renamed Nat's Track. Elizabeth Stevens's long-suffering aunty and uncle have died. Debbie Fream's partner Garry Blair was badly injured in a motorbike accident and died three years later; he was forty-three. Debbie and Garry's son Jake has always been in mourning. In 2018, he told the *Australian Women's Weekly*: 'I've lived my entire lifetime with what the killer did that night. He took everything from me. He took the happy life that was waiting for me.' Jake has also urged authorities to prevent the killer's release.

None of us who lived through those times will forget what the crimes did to our community. The judge got it right the first time.

For the record, the police case against me was downgraded to wilful damage, then dropped altogether. I never saw the inside of a courtroom. Higgo, Trav and I were in the clear after we paid the damages bill. That was it. No one from the school ever explained to me how this came to be. I found out the truth when I became a cadet newspaper reporter for the *Mordialloc-Chelsea News*. I had to go to the Chelsea cop shop to get snippets of police news from an officer called Senior-Sergeant Mike McInerney. He recognised me as the teenager who got locked up for breaking into his school. He explained that it was his decision to drop the charges. We were kids who deserved a second chance, he said.

Not long after school (and a few failed jobs), Adam moved to Queensland to chase his dreams of becoming a full-time singer. Then he went to Sydney, then Los Angeles, and dozens of cities in between. Along the way, he was signed with his three-piece pop band, Zinc, to a professional record deal and eventually made it into the Australian Top 40 Countdown. The album was called *Making Sense of Madness*.

We stayed in touch through emails and letters. I gave the best man's speech at his wedding in Mexico. Through tears, I told the guests how Adam and I had been mates since kindergarten. Almost everyone was drinking tequila after the ceremony. Not me. The smell reminded me of that messy night after I played under lights at the MCG. At the reception, Adam commented on how much I'd mellowed. 'You're so different to the kid you used to be,' he said. He sounded a bit concerned. I reassured him I was better off.

Not long after the wedding, Adam and his wife settled back into Seaford, five minutes from my house. They have two sons.

I moved away from home for about ten years. I got married at thirty and settled back in Seaford, bought a house, watched my three sons come into the world at Frankston Hospital, and started coaching the local football club. Seaford FC has changed a lot since the 1990s. It now has women's teams, and policies of respect and fairness. It has also retained its pride and community spirit. My brother is in charge of the Under 19 side. His coaching philosophy mirrors our father's.

My parents still live in the same house they built in 1977. They have twelve grandchildren and an empire of love that sustains us all. They celebrated their fiftieth wedding anniversary in 2020. They are my number one ranked heroes (Peter Daicos still holds a place in my top ten).

Hutchy went to the AFL after his stint at the Stingrays. He coached Melbourne for a while and spent time at other clubs in senior management roles. He's back making the moves as senior coach of amateur side Old Brighton Grammarians. His right-hand-man from 1993, Crouchy, died by suicide a couple of years after he was our fitness coach – the best I ever saw. I cannot fathom his death.

My old school Patterson River Secondary College is the other character in this book that has changed markedly in the past twenty-eight years. When I started going there in 1988, it was the kind of place where anything could happen, often for the worse. The school is now an institution of learning, respect and relative peace. My old Legal Studies teacher Mr O'Brien is still there, passionate as ever. I like to imagine how many children he has guided throughout the decades. Although I was banned from ever entering the schoolgrounds, I did go back. A few years ago, I attended a parents' tour. Mr O'Brien explained to me how much improvement he'd seen over the years. 'When you came here there was one fight a week,' he said. 'Now we'd see one a year.' My two eldest sons now attend Patterson River. Number three will join them in 2025. They are all better students than their father. They have the fire inside them. Like me, the boys have all benefitted from having a kind and inspirational mother.

In researching this book, I tracked down Mrs Mac. She was retiring as principal of a highly regarded country high school. We sat down for coffee. I asked her the one question I'd always wanted answered. 'Of all the books you could have chosen, why did you give me *I Heard the Owl Call My Name?*'

She said she thought I was showing signs of self-destruction in Year 12.

'Was I?'

'A little bit.' She smiled softly.

Mrs Mac told me the novel was a way of showing me there were other ways to be a man. I told her I found journalism because of her; that she helped save me.

My overwhelming gratitude belongs to all my good teachers. I was lucky to have them; I swear I'm crying writing this.

Another thing happened during the recent pandemic. Adam, Leigh and I found Doc. We hadn't seen each other since school. He drifted away and no one knew where he went. It turned out to be a happy story. Myles Maddock has made his home by the beach, with a beautiful family and good waves. We caught up on Zoom. All four of us together again in one place, albeit on a screen. We talked about our school days. Typically, Leigh spoke with an economy of words and quiet sense of humour. It was Doc, however, who summed up how we all felt about those years we spent side by side. 'I loved school,' he said. 'Because I had good friends. I had you guys.'

He was right. All those things that happened. All that uncertainty. All my fear. It was always going to work out. I had all I needed, all along.

As for playing footy, I still have dreams about getting ready to run out onto the MCG. Almost thirty years on. I had one the other night. I was in the change room, looking at myself in a mirror. I was old – like I am now. For some reason I started shadow boxing. Hutchy walked past me. He still looked the same. The coach wished me luck out there on the field. I caught him grinning. I felt calm, no tightness, only a few nerves. Ready. My teammates were coming and going from the bathroom and shouting about how we were going to win this game – this time we were going to have a bloody victory. The boys hadn't aged. They all had golden brown skin, curved biceps and shoulders, with perfect hair. I was the only one with grey hair, and I hoped no one noticed. Crouchy was there. He said it was time we started the game. Everyone ran out onto the oval and I went to join them. I was so happy – it was happening again – but I never made it out. The scene wouldn't alter. I stayed alone in the change room. The match started without me.

Acknowledgements

I'm grateful to Frankston Library for giving me access to its *Frankston Standard* and *The Independent* archives, and to the State Library of Victoria for its newspaper microfilm collection. I found *The Frankston Murders*, by Vikki Petraitis, especially helpful to my research. Kind thanks go to my outstanding and tireless editor Mic Looby, publisher Martin Hughes, agent Clare Forster and generous readers: Kim Stewart (formerly Mrs Mac), Tim Ayliffe, Joel Kennedy, Adam and Dad. Without my wife and sons, this book would never have made it. As always, Kim Kennedy was the first to read my work and encourage me to keep going. Jack, Gus and Leo patiently waited for my writing shifts to end before asking me to kick the footy with them on the road. My siblings Jo, Steve and Kate also deserve special mention. I have so many other wonderful memories of growing up together. I love you.